States of Architecture

in the Twenty-First Century

NEW DIRECTIONS FROM
THE SHANGHAI WORLD EXPO

States of Architecture
in the Twenty-First Century

NEW DIRECTIONS FROM
THE SHANGHAI WORLD EXPO

Rodolphe el-Khoury & Andrew Payne. Photographs by Nic Lehoux

table
of
contents.

012 Introduction.

018 Pavilions.

265 Documentation.

369 Appendix.

370 Credits.

376 Biographies.

Since the first world exhibition held in London in 1851, world fairs and expositions have been an important locus for the intersection of architectural invention, technological innovation, and the flows of transnational capital. Distinguished nineteenth century examples of this phenomenon include Joseph Paxton's "Crystal Palace", constructed for the Great Exhibition of 1851, and the Eiffel Tower, constructed thirty eight years later to serve as the entrance arch for the world exposition celebrating the centennial of the French Revolution. Mies van der Rohe's Barcelona Pavilion, constructed as the German Electrical Industries Pavilion for the World Expo held in Barcelona in 1929, and Iannis Xenakis/Le Corbusier's Philips Pavilion, constructed for the World Expo held in Brussels in 1958, speak to the persistence of this phenomenon in the century that followed.

Apart from its being the largest exhibition of its kind in world history (with an estimated 70 million people slated to attend), three things may be thought to distinguish the Shanghai Expo from its nineteenth and twentieth century precursors. First, this is arguably the first time that the global economy—of which world expos have always served as the anticipatory icons—is not merely a promise, but a realized fact. Second, it is unique among such exhibitions in taking the urban condition as its explicit theme. Finally, in this exposition the technological enthusiasm so very apparent in earlier expos is subject to a decidedly bioconstructive inflection, one informed not merely by concerns that architecture orchestrate a more 'sustainable' relationship between natural and technological systems, but also by a biomimetic impulse inspired by contemporary advances in the chemo-mechanical simulation of animate processes.

That Shanghai should serve as the host for the first world exhibition to explore the technological and cultural vicissitudes of a now globalized urban condition at the moment of China's emergence as a significant player in the new global economy is surely no accident. Shanghai has long served as a privileged site for commercial and cultural exchange between East and West. It was, we might say, a global city avant la lettre, and its significance as a world city with both a rich cosmopolitan past and a bright economic future is likely to increase as the economic and cultural consequences of globalization unfold.

Titled "Better City/Better Life", Shanghai Expo features contributions by more than 190 countries and 50 international organizations of one sort or another. In addition, there are several themed pavilions. Surveying the pavilions in their entirety, at least four themes or preoccupations begin to emerge: the first of these themes is biomimicry (a theme that must be related to a broader vitalist or neo-vitalist ethos in contemporary architecture). The second theme concerns the potentials of the architectural surface. Three things may be thought to characterize this second preoccupation: a neo-picturesque conception of the building as image rather than form; a sensualist aesthetic of wonder rather than of Kantian disinterest; and an eschewal of

any conception of the building façade as the syntactical assemblage of compositional elements in favour of an aesthetic of the micro-element whose indifferent repetition produces a textural or atmospheric field. The third overriding theme concerns the recalibration of the relationship between built object and landscape, a recalibration that seeks to render this relationship at once more pliable and more equivocal. In addition to the prevalence of these themes, one can observe the recurrence of a strategy that involves wrapping an informal constellation of at once programmatically and volumetrically diverse elements in a homogenous and regularly patterned membrane. This strategy serves to mediate between demands for programmatic complexity and spatial variety, on the one hand, and the need to offer an at once coherent and iconic presence to the street, on the other. In what follows, we will elaborate on these themes and strategies, showing how they emerge in various ways throughout the projects represented in this volume.

BIOMIMICRY

What is the "life" in "Better City / Better Life"? The historian and theorist of scientific culture, Eugene Thacker has described the Western conception of life as developing in three major episodes corresponding to three distinct models: life as soul (Aristotle), life as meat (Descartes) and life as pattern (the cybernetic conception of life as organized information). The idea of life arising from the cybernetic homology between living systems and information systems has had a strong hold on the contemporary architectural imagination for several decades (in no small part owing to the ubiquity of computer aided design).

This cybernetic conception of life has powerfully influenced the contemporary conception of the building as an animate or quasi-animate entity. Since the early nineties, that conception can be said to have advanced in three stages: the first stage (represented by the work of architects like Bernard Cache and Greg Lynn) imagined the building form as the empirical trace of a process of virtual morphogenesis. The second stage, represented by architects like MY STUDIO / Howeler+Yoon, Khoury Levit Fong, and Mark Goulthorpe, exploited the potentials of embedded technologies to re-conceive the built work as artificial sensorium. At the third stage, largely enabled by digital parametric modeling, the building is conceived, in conformity with Thacker's third paradigm (life=pattern), as the aggregate produced by the patterning of micrological elements.

These stages are less consecutive than cumulative, since strong residues of the earlier stages can be observed in even the most daring and radical examples of the later ones. In the Shanghai Expo, vestiges of all three are apparent, although it is perhaps the fascination with the patterns produced by the dense but carefully regulated distribution of a micro-element across a surface or field that produces the most novel

and ingenious expressions of this vitalism. It is here, also, that these vitalist preoccupations begin to encroach on our second theme, surface.

The treatment of both the interior and exterior surfaces of the U.K. Pavilion are ex-
emplary in this regard. The Seed Cathedral, situated at the centre of a deftly terraced
landscape, consists of a steel and timber composite structure pierced by 60,000 fibre
optic filaments, 20 mm square in section, which are encased in aluminum sleeves.
By day, the filaments draw daylight inward to illuminate the building's interior,
while at night light sources within the rods illuminate them so that the whole structure glows. Perhaps one of the most fascinating dimensions of this surface is
its capacity to be affected by changes in the surrounding milieu. Not only do the
filaments on the exterior skin move like hair when touched by even the gentlest of
passing breezes, their sensitivity to changes of light allows them to register, through
changes in the luminosity of the filament tips that stud the interior skin, the movement of clouds overhead.

This strategy of employing a dense patterning of micro-elements to form a continuous and evenly variegated surface or constellation of surfaces has sometimes been
viewed as a counter response to the postmodern tendency to understand the architectural artifact in semiotic terms, as a kind of visual symbol or sign. However, in the
Korean Pavilion, the repetition of the micro-element threatens to collapse the differ-
ence between ornamental form and semantic content, geometric pattern and syn-
tactic sequence. In this building, the exterior surfaces are produced through the patterned alteration of two types of pixel. The first type consists of white panels bearing
a relief of Han-guel letters rendered in a range of sizes; the second type consists of
works by the Korean artist Ik-Joon Kang, renowned for his massive art walls made
from hand painted tiles. The alteration of these panels produces a kind of pixelation
of the building's surface, transforming its complex figure into the armature for a
Borgesian landscape populated by symbols flickering enigmatically between pattern
element and semiotic cipher.

SURFACE: FROM FAÇADE TO INTERFACE TO SPECIAL EFFECTS MACHINE

Our discussion of the biomimetic impulse at play in the works populating this exhibition has already signaled the prominence of surface in the contemporary orchestration
of architecture's effects. As many of the pavilions show, digital technologies have had
a significant role to play in this development. That role concerns not merely a significant extension of the range of what is feasible, it also concerns a fundamental shift
(or sequence of shifts) in our conception of what a surface is and how it mediates our
relations with one another and with our surroundings. We might describe that shift as
involving the transformation of our conception of the surface as façade into a conception of the surface as interface, a movement, then, from surface as the instrument of

social and spatial differentiation to surface as the conduit for mediated connection. More recently another paradigm has emerged: the surface as special effects machine. Interestingly, the first significant example of this surface strategy was another piece of exposition architecture, Diller and Scofidio's Blur Pavilion for the Swiss Expo in 2002. Inspired no doubt in part by the Blur Pavilion, artificially produced clouds, mists, and spectra of various sorts are plentiful in recent architecture, and that plenty is very adequately represented in the submissions to this exposition. An interesting example is the Corporate Pavilion, whose surfaces are outfitted with an array of sensors and actuators that allow them to respond to the site's immediate conditions in a way productive of both aesthetic and ecological amenity. For instance, misters embedded in the building's external skin respond to increases in heat by emitting a cloud of cooling vapour. The vapour serves to both augment environmental performance and to enhance the foamy character of the façade.

Such effects are not exclusive to electronic media. The Spanish Pavilion achieves similar ecological goals and atmospheres with a meshwork of tubular steel and 8,524 wicker shingles. Intricately layered natural fibers deployed in a complex curvilinear form here modulate light and shade to define and shelter gathering spaces.

BUILDING AS LANDSCAPE/LANDSCAPE AS BUILDING

Landscape architecture has enjoyed an unprecedented prominence in recent discussions of architecture, serving not only as a disciplinary pursuit in its own right, but also as a model for reimagining the future of built architecture and urban design in view of new cultural and ecological circumstances.

This prominence is the result of a variety of factors, among which are to be numbered landscape architecture's traditional role as mediator between the natural and the artificial systems and elements that comprise the human environment. Not surprisingly, then, the cybernetically inflected vitalism that we observed in our brief discussion of biomimetic strategies is also a factor in the contemporary prominence of landscape, where it is associated with the application of terms and paradigms originating in systems ecology to the interpretation and construction of the built environment.

If the prominence of landscape in a wide array of pavilions can be indexed to this cyber-naturalism, it is also symptomatic of an interest in reimagining the relationship of building to site in such a way as to produce novel interlacings of interiority and exteriority, object and milieu. In order to give some sense of the variety of strategies deployed in aid of these interests, we will briefly discuss three pavilions: the Expo Pavilion, the U.K. Pavilion, and the French Pavilion.

In what might be seen as a discreet nod to the tectonic features of the pavilion as a building type consisting of a constellation of vertical members topped by a textile canopy, the Expo Pavilion is in essence a colossal roof structure lofted on 50 giant masts whose support is buttressed by 6 steel and glass framework shells. Reminiscent of the lightweight construction of Frei Otto's design for the German Pavilion of Expo '67, the structure frees sightlines and pedestrian movement while serving as both a hovering icon of virtuoso engineering and a monumental diagram of the distribution of program across the site. In addition, spacious lateral slopes flood the floor levels with light and air. The result is a building both maximally open to and imbedded in its surroundings.

The U.K. building can be thought to orchestrate an entirely distinct approach to the relationship of building to landscape, one wherein the interaction of building and site is defined by a clear differentiation of roles. The pavilion is a kind of two-part invention, in which the first part consists of the Seed Cathedral whose ingenious surface effects have already been described, and the second part consists of a carefully terraced landscape comprised of surfaces covered with artificial grass. In sharp contrast to the hard ground surface of the adjacent sites, these surfaces are designed to continue the texture of the Seed Cathedral's interior and exterior surfaces as well as to offer a welcoming public space for visitors to sit and view the building. Canopied and naturally ventilated entrance and exit sequences provide a circulation zone along three sides of the site. That zone contains three installations by the London-based design firm Troika: Green City, Open City, and Living City.

Despite the conspicuousness of a cosmopolitan spirit fueled by global capital and technological virtuosity, expressions of national pride are a constituent feature of world expositions, and the Shanghai exposition is no exception. Perhaps the most architecturally consequential of these nationalist expressions is to be found in the French Pavilion, where a celebration of the restrained sensualism that has traditionally distinguished the Gallic expression of neo-classical values finds a surprisingly contemporary expression.

As was the case with the U.K. Pavilion, the relationship between building and site is clearly differentiated. The familiar type of the courtyard building with a classical French garden at its centre, a type which arguably finds its apotheosis in Claude Perrault's library with interior court, is here subject to an unexpectedly picturesque inflection, reconceived as a succession of atmospherically and programmatically distinct episodes unfolding along a continuous ramp that twists around the court garden before terminating in a roof garden. That succession reveals a taut dialectic between the symmetry and decorous regularity of the court garden and the dense mélange of media presentations and atmospheric effects that animate the galleries strung along the ramp. The French spirit of the pavilion is also revealed in the intricately carved topiary that extends from the roof garden into the court below.

The photographs within this book were produced by Architectural Photographer Nic Lehoux over 8 sessions in the early days of Expo 2010. Some of them were commissioned directly by the architects, others were chosen as part of this photoessay. They seek not to represent the entire documentation of the site and all its pavilions, but to create a concise photoessay of some of the most architecturally significant and innovative pavilions that were designed for the world fair.

Significantly, Nic's photographs differ largely from those produced at Expo by his unique combination of extremely rigorous composition and lighting and a relative freeform, whimsical blurred depiction of the masses visiting the pavilions on the popular site. The methods Nic applies to his Architectural work were thus translated into a document of artistic merit outside of the realm of traditional architectural photography.

74.france

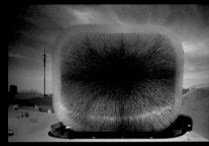
84.uk.

160.germany

180.german-chinese house

20.expo axis

38.chile

50.spain

110.finland

118.denmark

148.luxembourg

196.uae.

202.south korea

230.shanghai corporate

expo axis.

*SBA design
Stuttgart / Shanghai.*

This pavilion is one of the five permanent structures. It is meant to become a public amenity for the new urban district that is slated for development on the Expo site. The design is by the Stuttgart-based firm that won an international competition for this prestigious commission. The building is one of the most important of the exposition, marking the entrance and defining the main axis of the site. It is also the most ambitious in terms of technological innovation and sheer magnitude.

The building is a tour de force of engineering. Its tensile roof structure spans 100 meters, pushing the envelope of what is feasible with the technology. The roof membrane is propped on a series of colossal masts and held in tension with massive anchors that attach to the structure underneath. The funnel shaped anchor resonates with the geometry of the Sun Valleys: oversized glass and steel masts that bring light to the lower decks and provide shelter under their flaring caps.

The juxtaposition of the funnel-shaped anchors and masts offers a striking composition where fabric in tension and glass and steel in compression are rhetorically compared and contrasted.

BSA was partnered with Knippers Helbig Advanced Engineering Stuttgart for the innovative design and engineering. Together they continue a German tradition of lightweight construction that developed with Frei Otto's groundbreaking works. Much like the German Pavilion at the World Exposition 1967 in Montreal and the Munich Olympic stadium—formative precedents that defined the genre—the Expo Axis shows how advanced computation and material research align to produce structures of increasing elegance and efficiency.

The Expo Axis is the largest building on the
Expo site with 350,000 m2 of useable space.

The roof structure lives up to Stuttgart's
tradition of lightweight construction.

Six funnel-shaped structures, the 'Sun Valleys',
direct natural light into the lower levels.

The building is a gateway to the 1 km long and 100 m wide avenue that leads to the theme-based pavilions.

The superstructure is supported on nine mega-columns including glass and steel funnels.

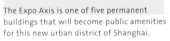
The Expo Axis is one of five permanent
buildings that will become public amenities
for this new urban district of Shanghai.

chile.

Sabbagh Arquitectos.

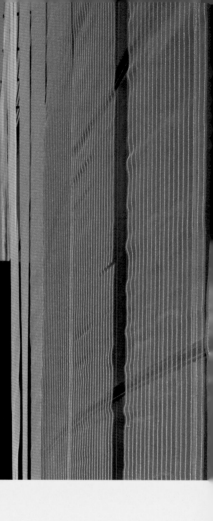

The pavilion condenses elements of the urban experience in the interplay of discrete programmed rooms and open free flowing public paths and spaces. It consists mainly of a large amoeba-shaped space intersected by contrasting prismatic volumes. The curvilinear envelope is translucent; its layers of recyclable glass and steel mesh are designed for generous day-lighting and heat-gain control. It partially unveils the inner life of the building to the street, especially at night when the entire pavilion glows like a lantern. The opaque and crisply edged volumes offer a sharp contrast in their monolithic character; they are clad in self-weathering steel panels. The plan of the pavilion enables open ended, unscripted activity while also setting up a rich promenade that strings the themed hermetic rooms along a ramping path. Each room constitutes an episode in an unfolding narrative that culminates in the so-called "Seed" room. Here the main thrust of the Pavilion's theme is brought home: a vision of the city's human face and dedications. The *pièce de résistance* of the pavilion is the "Main Square" where a striking atmospheric effect is orchestrated with variations in the use of richly textured wood cladding and overhead lighting filtered through a diaphanous ceiling. This space is a monument to wood construction, showcasing in myriad varieties and applications of Chilean pine the potential of wood as a building material. Most importantly it underscores the architectural and environmental relevance of a material that is light, renewable and recyclable.

A translucent curvilinear envelope of layered glass and steel meshwork unifies the ambitious program of Chile's Pavilion.

The wood-clad ramp leading
and exiting the med rooms.

Pillars, beams and roof trusses are bolted in place to facilitate the assembly and later dismantling of the building.

Floor, ceiling and wall cladding is of renewable
Chilean pine in a variety of available products:
plywood, laminated boards and solid wood elements.

Wooden ramps emulating
urban streets.

spain.

Benedetta Tagliabue.

A basket-like structure envelops the open and enclosed spaces of the Spanish pavilion. It shapes the building and defines its character while sheltering from the sun, dust and noise. The intricately textured surface is a tubular steel structure with a complex curvilinear geometry that is clad with 8524 wicker panels arranged in a shingle pattern. The alignment of digital technology with artisanal craft here makes a persuasive case for the recovery of vernacular charm and efficiency with high-tech means and ingenuity.

The Pavilion, designed by Benedetta Tagliabue of the firm Miralles Tagliabue Architects, speaks eloquently about the coordination of low and high-tech means in ways that take advantage of new methods of fabrication in a new global economy. The tubular steel structure is modeled and fabricated with the help of sophisticated software that rationalizes its complex double curvatures for efficient production and assembly. The wicker panels belong to the basket-making field, a thriving artisanal tradition with a global reach.

The steel structure with its curvilinear inflections enables the large spanning sweeps of the sheltering wall. The infinitely varied wickerwork, creates with the richness, intelligence and unparalleled intricacy of handmade products an atmosphere that is reminiscent of Hispanoarabic architecture with its play of light and shade, transparency and opacity.

The combined effects of freeform contours with intricately layered natural fibers, a sustainable material par excellence, create a unique architecture that is both traditional and progressive, demonstrating new possibilities for responsible and efficient uses of resources in sustainable and livable cities.

Nicknamed by Chinese media as the "Spanish
basket", the pavilion uses 8,524 wicker panels to
clad its tubular steel structure.

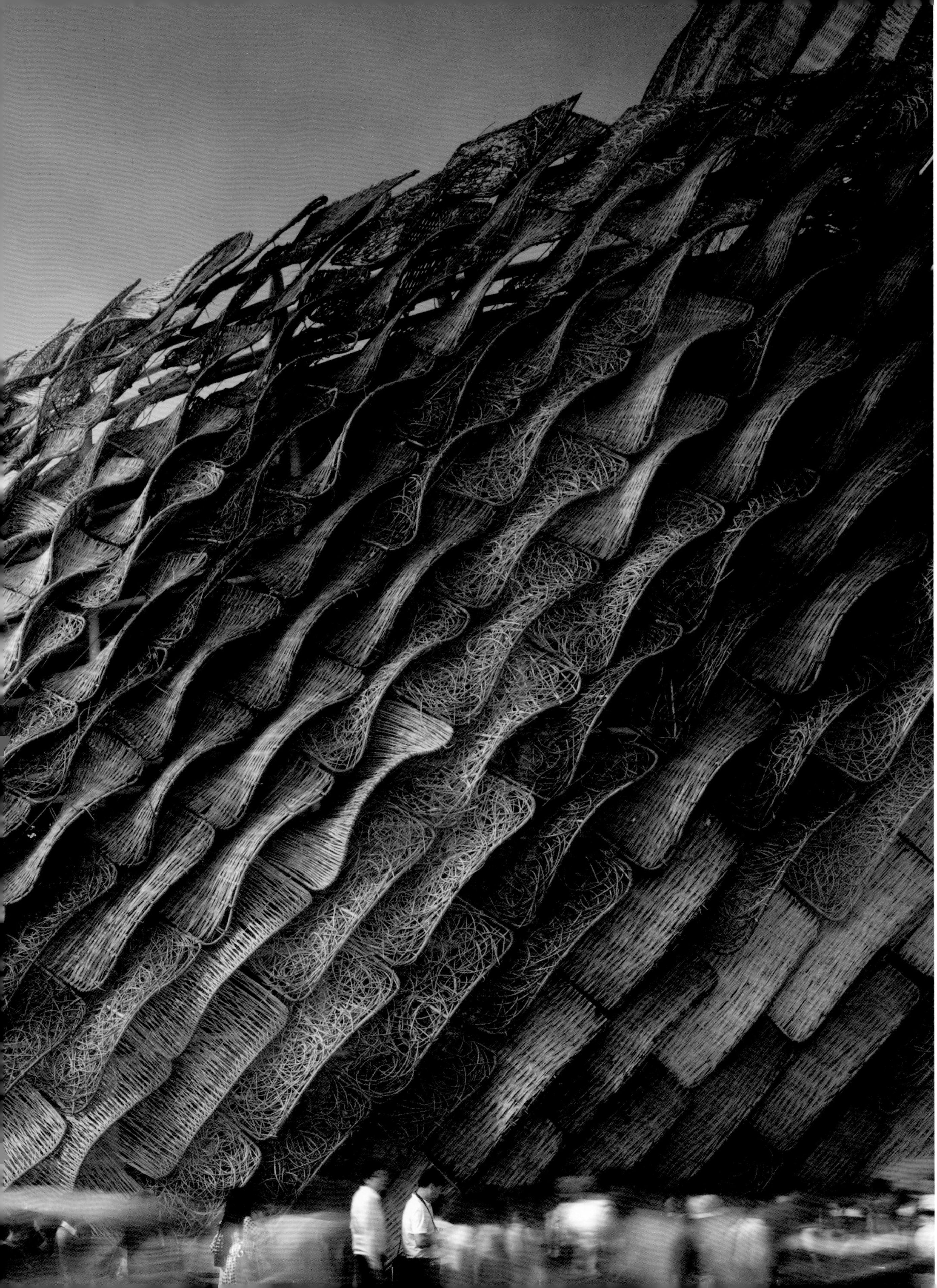

The wicker is coated in a water-proofing compound
that is well suited to Shanghai's heavy precipitation.

The Spanish Pavilion hosts a Tapas Bar, multiple conference rooms, an official reception hall and a 150 occupant multi-functional auditorium.

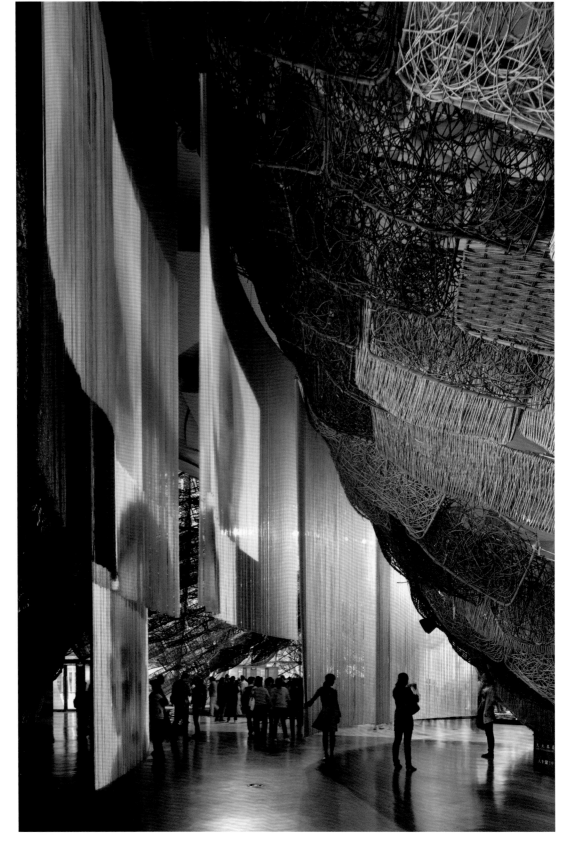

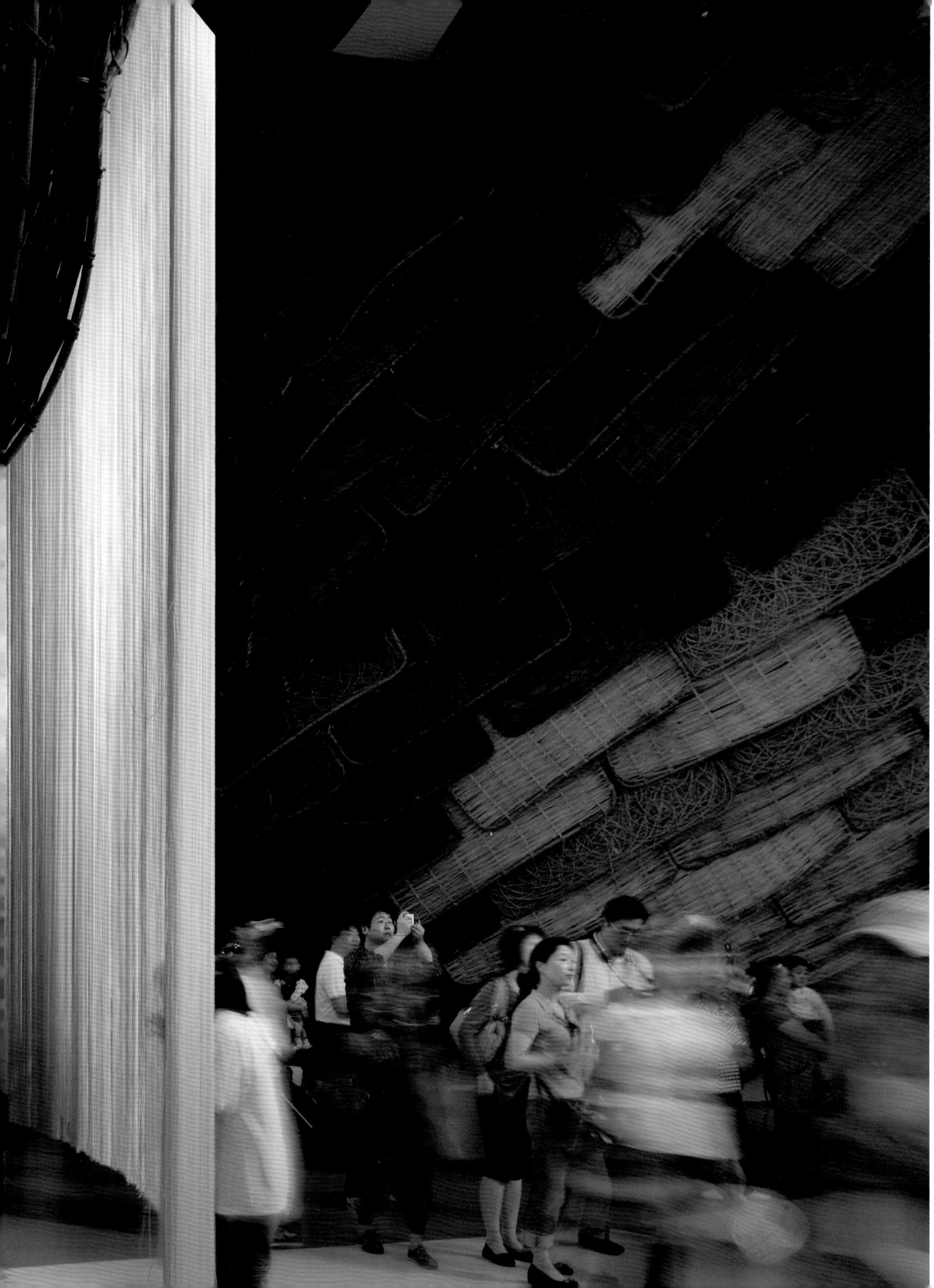

Spiral stairs and ramps allow easy
and fluid passage

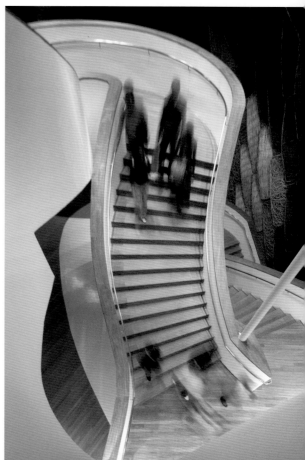

Sinuous lines combine to align the warmth
of organic materials with new technology.

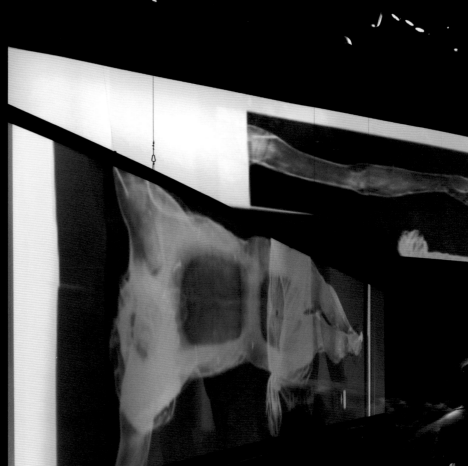

Audio-visual shows in multiple screens
take place inside the pavilion.

The "Spanish basket" at diferent hours
in the night

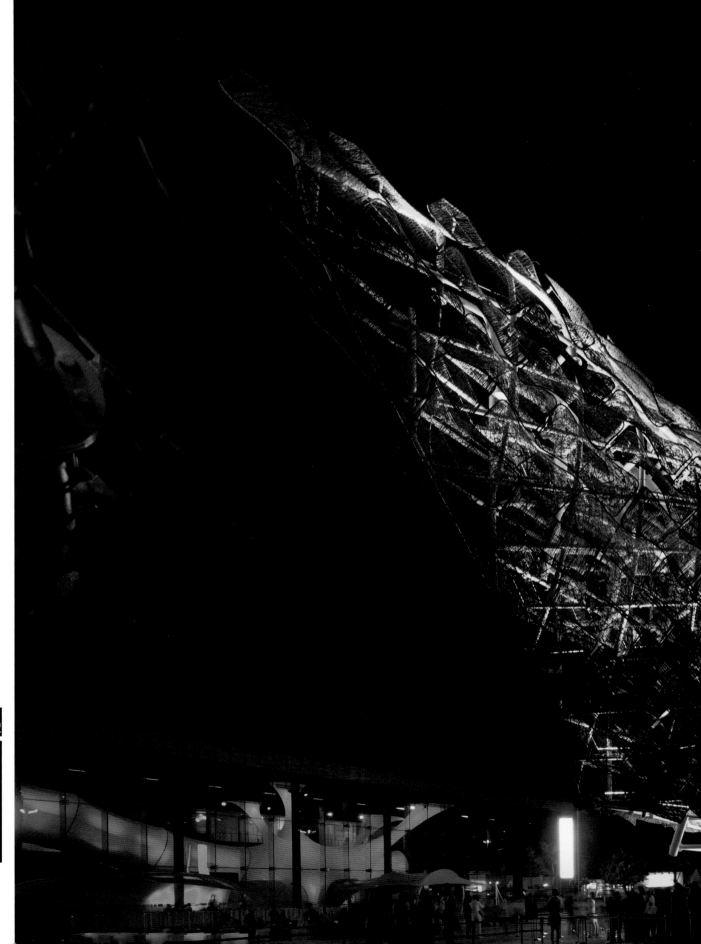

france.

Jacques Ferrier Architectures.

The French pavilion aims to recreate the sensory world of France with installations targeting all the senses for a fully immersive experience. The building stages within a stately package a series of experiences in a continuous multi-media circuit featuring highlights from French cinema classics, samples of perfumes and ambient noises of Paris, to name just a few of the many effects that create the French ambience throughout.

The building primarily consists of a continuous ramp that rises within a structural shell around a square court and terminates in a roof garden. Intricately carved topiary cascades from the roof into the courtyard covering the interior elevations in a thick layer of living ornament.

The living wall, along with other eco-friendly features rhetorically integrated into the spatial and decorative makeup of the building overtly state the environmental dedications of the building. The precisely etched topiary is most effective in demonstrating the potential of living systems as building material while embracing the long established French tradition of a geometricized and rationalized nature.

The green court, the physical and 'spiritual' core of the structure, is in constant visual focus from the gently ascending galleries. Its regularity and symmetry contrast with the animated and ever-changing ambience. The parametric compression of its diagrid toward the top—perhaps a reference to proportional inflections in French classical architecture—yields subtle variations in component geometry and assembly that speak to the sophistication of CNC parametric modeling and fabrication.

The densely landscaped courtyard-type building features living walls with topiary cascading down from the roof garden into the atrium.

Fountains and living green walls help in cooling the main outdoor space. Screen walls control the light inside.

The France Pavilion seemingly floats
above surrounding reflective pools.

Concrete lattice work encasing the building.

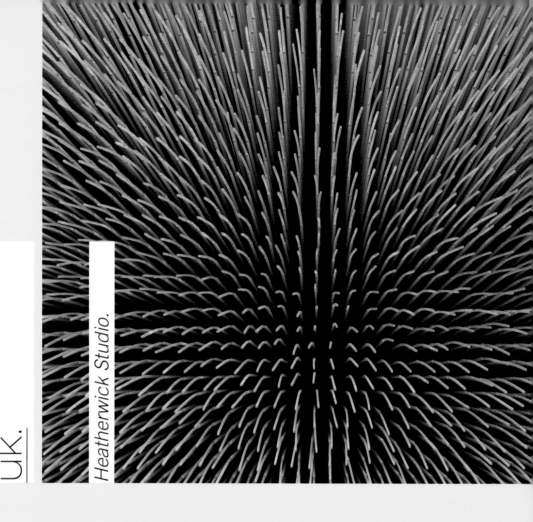

uk.

Heatherwick Studio.

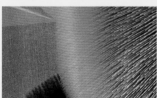

Working with the Kew Gardens Millennium Seedbank, Thomas Heathwick Studio designed a pavilion consisting of two main elements, the Seed Cathedral, a biomorphic icon situated at the centre of the site, and the multi-layered 6,000 m2 landscape that surrounds it. Designed to be a direct manifestation of the thing it exhibits (a collection of thousands of seeds culled from China's Kunming Institute of Botany, a partner in the Millennium Seedbank Project), the Seed Cathedral is a steel and timber structure pierced by 60,000 fibre-optic filaments, 20mm in section, which pass through aluminum sleeves. The dense aggregation of these filaments then forms both the exterior and the interior surfaces of the building. From the outside the building resembles nothing so much as a giant sea anemone. From the interior it appears as a kind of cave or grotto illuminated by a hovering galaxy of luminious studs, each containing one of the seeds. By day, the filaments draw daylight inward to illuminate the building's interior, while at night light sources within the rods illuminate them so that the whole structure glows. The filaments also serve as devices for making the cathedral highly responsive to even the smallest events in its immediate environment. Not only do the filaments on the exterior skin move like hair when touched by even the gentlest of passing breezes, their sensitivity to changes of light allows them to register, through changes in the luminosity of the filament tips that stud the interior skin, the movement of clouds overhead.

The second part of the pavilion is a generous, multi-layered open space paved with an artificial grass that is both an extension of the visual idiom of the building's internal and external skins and a sharp contrast with the surfaces that pave adjacent sites. The open space gives room for visitors to stop and rest, but also provides multiple unobstructed views of the Cathedral. Canopied and naturally ventilated entrance and exit sequences provide a circulation zone along three sides of the site. That zone contains three installations by the London-based design firm Troika: Green City, Open City, and Living City.

The 6,000 m2 site is treated as a multi-layered landscape with the Seed Cathedral as a focal point.

The Seed Cathedral comprises 60,000 7.5 meter long
fibre-optic rods encasing seeds at their tips.

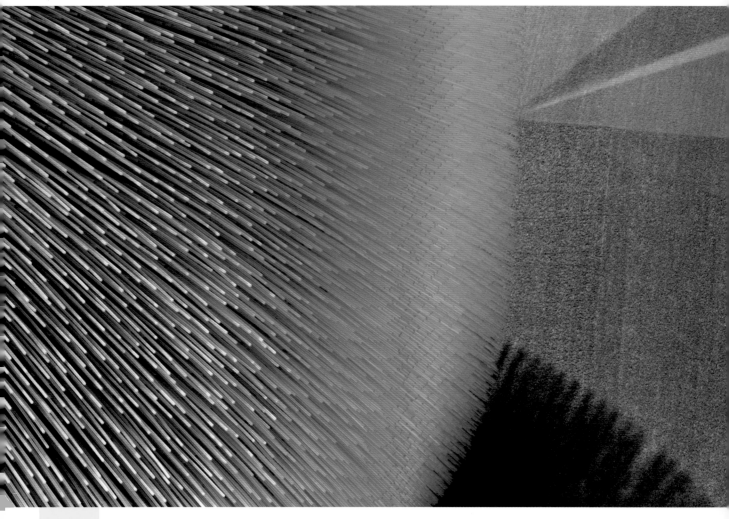

Fibre-optic rods.

The Seed Cathedral has a steel and timber composite
structure supporting a fur-like array of plastic rods.

The fibre-optic filaments are particularly
responsive to changing external light conditions.

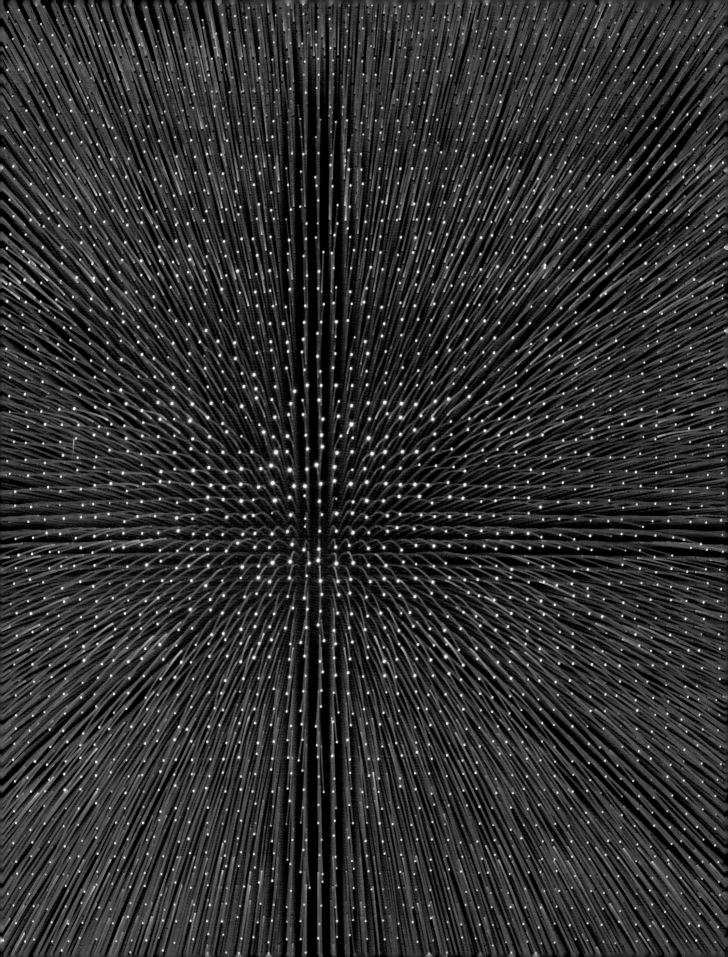

At night the whole structure glows
with the light transmitted through the
clear plastic rods.

The solemn atmosphere of the Seed
Cathedral's inner sanctum.

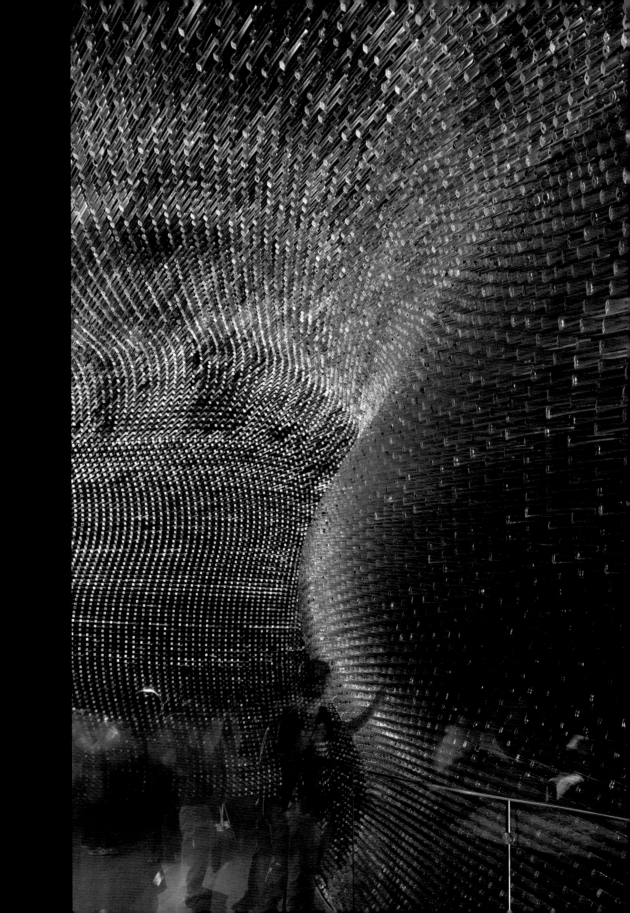

The tips of the fibre-optic filaments constitute a floating galaxy of mini-vitrines for a vast collection of seeds.

Visitors are surrounded by tens of thousands of seeds in glowing plastic cases.

The pavilion at night

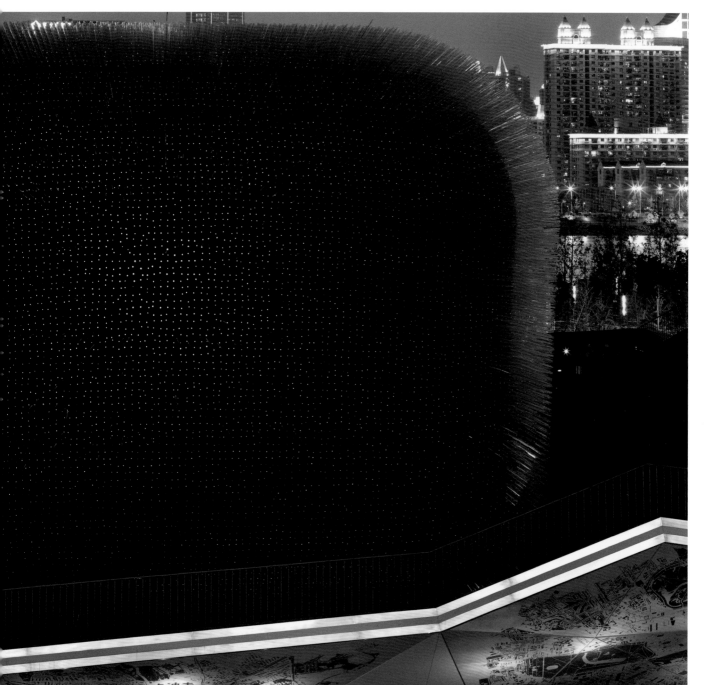

finland.

JKMM Architects.

The Finnish pavilion is titled "Kirnu", which translates as "Giant's Kettle": a metaphorical crucible where ideas are gathered and mixed. It has a minimal sculptural form that is meant to evoke abstract ideas such as "freedom, creativity, and innovation," as well as elements of Finland's rocky landscape.

It is basically a courtyard building with exhibition spaces and meeting rooms packed in an ascending trajectory around a pristine atrium: a blank canvas and forum for public gatherings at the heart of the pavilion.

The design by the Helsinki-based architect's office JKMM emphasizes the Finnish dedication to sustainable development. The architects gave particular attention to the pavilion's lifecycle, building into the structure a potential for expansion and adaptive reuse. The choice of materials and construction methods extends the building's lifespan while ingenious design solutions facilitate assembly and disassembly. The form of the building is calibrated for optimal sun exposure and ventilation. Recycled materials, operable windows and ventilating flues also minimize CO_2 emissions. The character-defining feature of the elevation proclaims the pavilion's environmental mandate: a scale-like shingle made of recycled paper and plastic.

The minimalist form of the pavilion's atrium.

A gently sloping ramp ascends within the thick walls of Kirnu toward the exhibition hall, a grand space that winds around the atrium.

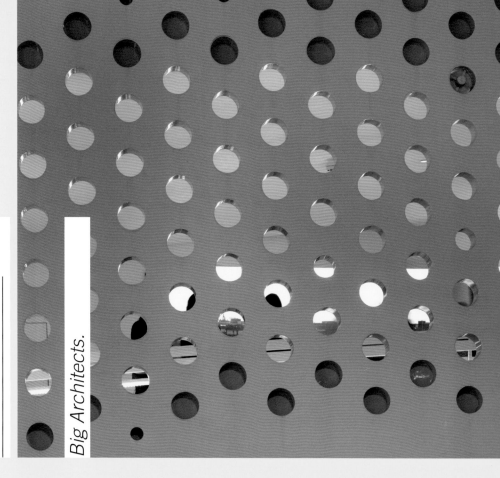

denmark.

Big Architects.

The building aims to recreate situations and experiences that are reminiscent of Copenhagen. It restages in their distilled essences some of the city's characteristic conditions, invites visitors to partake of typical Danish activities and puts them in direct contact with authentic icons. In designer Bjarke Ingels' own words: "You can ride the city bike, take a swim in the harbor pool, and see the real Little Mermaid."

The building is a continuous ramp optimized in two intertwined loops for the flow of city bikes and pedestrians. It belongs to a genealogy of buildings epitomized by Rem Koolhaas' Jussieu Library that seek to animate the city and enhance the urban experience with the architectural orchestration and facilitation of public flows. The aim here is to distance the building from the discrete pavilion type and its institutional monumentality to become a seamless extension of the Expo's public street and pedestrian walkway. This obstacle-free architecture is particularly welcoming to bicycles: the pavilion offers 300 city-bicycles to use at no charge on the pavilion's exhibition circuit and elsewhere on the Expo site as a sample of Danish city life and a sustainable mode of transportation.

The pavilion has an abstract sculptural quality that is enhanced by the monolithic steel construction. Reflective white paint aids in cooling the building along with perforations on the external steel-plated walls. The perforation pattern, also inspired by Koolhaas' work, namely the inbuilt Prada store in San Francisco, is derived from stress analysis diagrams. It translates the invisible forces that keep the building up into a tangible image.

The pavilion is bike-friendly,
much like a Danish city.

The blue cycle path and white concrete
surfaces designate the arrival and exit areas.

In the harbor pool at the centre of the pavilion, the
authentic Little Mermaid is on loan for this exhibition.

Inside, the floor is covered with light epoxy and the characteristic blue that defines Denmark's cycle paths.

Pedestrian circuit

The width of the loop varies and is defined
by the program of the inner space.

Visitors are invited to experience some of Copenhagen's best attractions: the city bike, the harbor pool, a picnic on the roof garden and the opportunity to see the authentic Little Mermaid.

Over 300 free city bikes available on the roofscape, offer the visitors a chance to experience the Danish urban lifestyle.

Looping circuits manage the
flow through the pavilion.

Navigating the pavilion's ramps

Interior loop with night-
time illumination

luxembourg.

Hermann & Valentiny.

The pavilion, a castle-like structure with an intensely planted landscape, translates into built form the Chinese word for Luxembourg "lùsên bâo", which literally means forest and castle. The composition, with a fortress-like but permeable wall is also an allegory of Luxembourg's position in the world: a small and proud nation open to global and fertile exchanges. The towering structure within the precinct is a caricature of a typical single family home, the basic building block of Luxembourg's urban environment. It houses the cultural program of the pavilion. The perimeter wall, fortress-like in appearance but entirely permeable to the flow of visitors, is dedicated to business oriented programs.

Architects Hermann & Valentiny here give particular attention to the integration of plant material. Extensive planters transform the pavilion's walls into a living architecture while a heavily planted courtyard brings nature to the heart of the building.

The 'forest and fortress' idea comes from the literal meaning of the Chinese word for Luxembourg.

Views of pavilion interiors

germany.

Schmidhuber + Kaindl.

The German Pavilion entitled "Balancity" seeks to metaphorically communicate an idea of the diverse forces that shape the city with their precariously balanced interactions. It consists of four discrete and intricately shaped volumes that rely on each other to collectively achieve structural stability.

The structurally interdependent volumes together constitute a canopy that protects a hybrid landscape that intertwines interior and exterior spaces; buildings and gardens and urban and rural references. The strange and familiar landscape captures the de-fining contradictions of the contemporary city and its capacity to absorb and reconcile nature and artifice, leisure and production, density and open space.

The building orchestrates the trajectory of visitors through the heterogeneous and animated landscape in a promenade that culminates in a vertical amphitheater dedicated to a multi-media spectacle, the *pièce de résistance* of the media-saturated environment. Visitors reach the pavilion's spacious event-area via a spiraling set of staircases from the 'Energy Source'.

Four structures create a large canopy over a hybrid landscape of natural and architectural features.

Access to one of the individual structures

The German pavilion is an inhabitable sculpture representing the complex ecology of the city.

Roof gardens

Visitors move along a variety of pathways
including moving walkways.

Installations inside the pavillions.

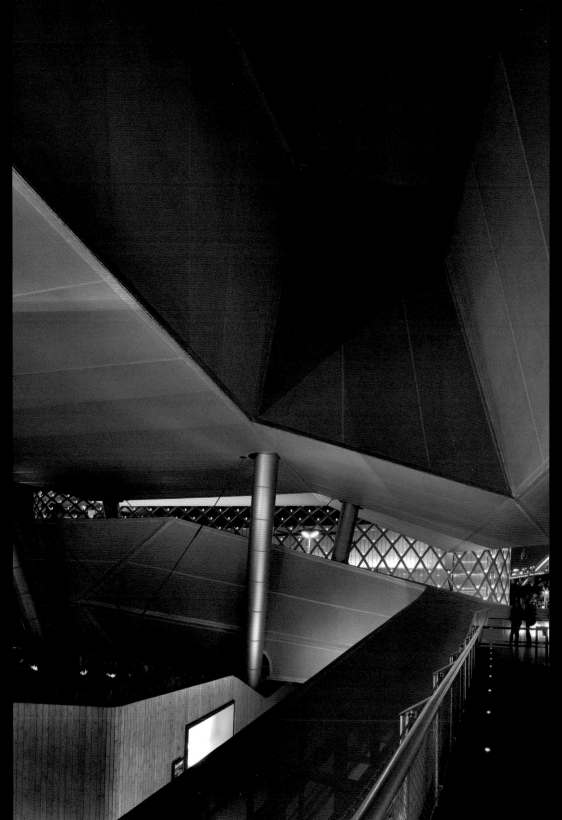

Animated interior landscape

Interplay of interior and
exterior spaces

german-chinese house.

Markus Heinsdorff.

This pavilion is the culmination of the event series "Germany and China – Moving Ahead Together," a three-year program that showcases the products of a Chinese-German collaboration in sustainable development. The pavilion is a masterful demonstration of the use of light and renewable resources in large buildings. The structure is almost entirely made of bamboo, a plant that is environmentally friendly and particularly efficient in its frugal use of resources. Bamboo has a considerable advantage over wood in its fast rate of renewal, with a growth of up to 30 centimeters per day. Most importantly, it's a material that combines the benefits of lightness, elasticity and hardness in equal measure: characteristics that are particularly suited for a load-bearing structure. The building rhetorically showcases the structural virtues of bamboo and eloquently reveals its potential as a noble material that is suited for institutional and monumental applications.

The pavilion was designed by Markus Heinsdorff, a designer/artist whose work aligns traditional materials and building methods with high-tech means and sophistication. He mobilizes cutting-edge techniques of modeling and fabrication while capitalizing on the intelligence sedimented in natural materials and processes to create structures that combine the efficiency of nature with the ingenuity of engineering.

Heinsdorff thus combines the natural rigidity of bamboo with the stiffening effect of pleated surfaces to enhance the structural integrity of the pavilion's monumental walls. The building evokes the vernacular tradition of bamboo construction in China yet it is unmistakably a building of the present. It speaks a modern language that is replete with formal inventions derived from advanced computational modeling in geometry and stress analysis.

The structure is made of Julong
bamboo, a rare and particularly
tall variety from South China.

The upper story is integrated
into the structure.

消防栓

The roof surfaces and supporting beams are reminiscent of bamboo fans or paper umbrellas.

The building is environment-friendly and
mobile: it is designed for easy transportation
and assembly/disassembly.

Materials are either reusable
or recyclable.

CNC-fabricated steel joinery

uae.

Foster + Partners.

Foster + Partners based the geometry of the UAE pavilion on the form of sand dunes. The architects transposed the climate-based logic that shapes the dunes to emphasize solar exposure rather than wind. Much like a sand dune, the pavilion is smooth and gently sloping on one side—the one that would be subjected to prevailing wind forces—and intricately textured on the protected, more vertical side. The sloping smooth side here shields the building from southern solar exposure while the northern elevation is permeable to daylight and fresh air.

The pavilion is assembled from stainless steel flat panels that are tessellated in a variegated pattern. The geometry and building method is designed to facilitate the transportation of building components and on-site assembly. It was developed with the use of state-of-the-art parametric modeling and fabrication techniques to optimize the use of material and labor resources.

The building is primarily dedicated to meeting the environmental agenda of the Expo and showcasing the UAE's progressive stance on sustainability. A central feature is an exhibit of the groundbreaking Masdar Initiative, an on-going project for a 6 million square meter carbon neutral zero waste community in Abu Dhabi.

The UAE pavilion embodies the environmental intelligence built into the natural desert landscape while adapting it to new materials and methods of construction. Its iconic form evokes the characteristic feature that unites the seven emirates and their traditions while its high-tech constitution progressively projects architecture into an environment friendly future.

The sand dune-inspired pavilion references physical
and symbolic features shared by all seven emirates.

The structure is a triangulated lattice of flat stainless steel panels designed for easy assembly/disassembly.

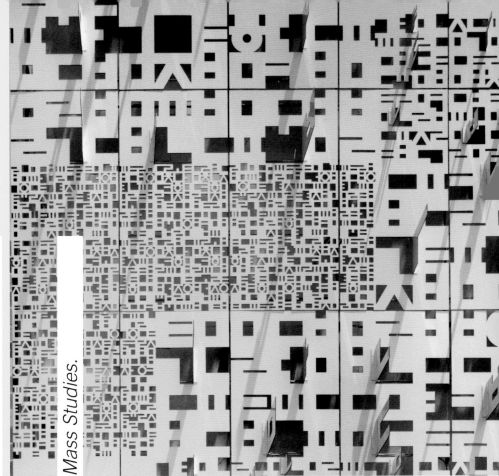

south korea.

Mass Studies.

The Korean pavilion looks like a low-resolution picture of a building. It is clad with panels of varying size designed and conceived as physical pixels that aggregate into larger figures or break down into individual bits. The design, by Seoul-based Mass Studies, is consistent with current trends that capitalize on the potential of digital parametric modeling and fabrication techniques to aggregate infinitely varied building blocks into complex architectural constellations. The method imitates the processes by which morphological complexity in nature grows from the accretion and variegation of simple constituent parts. It also captures, and translates into a memorable image, the informational constitution of architecture and the extent to which contemporary buildings are shaped and produced by digital media. The orchestration of pixels and figure is also related to the Korean culture and language. The form of the pavilion is based on Han-geul, the Korean alphabet, with graphic symbols aggregated and translated into special constructs. The building envelope is clad in a variety a square panels—physical pixels that coalesce in myriad combina-

tions. The white variety features Han-geul symbols. The colored 'art pixels', are 45 cm x 45 cm aluminum panels created by Ik-Joong Kang, a Korean artist known for his mosaic-like murals.

The intricately woven patterns of Han-geul and art pixels create a variety of effects that are both atmospheric and symbolic: visitors are immersed in a rich texture of shifting colors, light and patterns while they decode the ever-shifting programmed messages that animate the elevation with back-lit Han-geul pixels.

Within the three-dimensional matrix of concatenated symbols the pavilion offers a variety of space for small-group meetings and large public gatherings including a 40 m x 77 m landscape extending under the pavilion's lifted volumes. The landscape is an abstract translation of a typical Korean city, complete with a miniaturized mountain and river for visitors to enjoy while queuing for the programmed spaces above. Much like the rest of the building, this public room bathes in the atmosphere of digitality, saturated with flickering pixels, both virtual and physical.

Using 'convergence' as the main theme, the South Korea Pavilion collapses notions of 'sign' and 'space' into a three-dimensional symbol.

The exterior surfaces of the Korea Pavilion are clad in pixel-like aluminum panels.

Visitors enjoy the landscape while
queuing for the exhibits above.

Art Pixels are 45 cm x 45 cm aluminum panels
created by the Korean artist, Ik-Joong Kang.

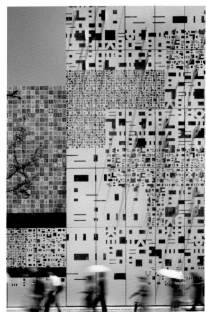

Variegated surfaces create
changing atmospheres.

Han-geul Pixels are white panels with
letters from the Korean alphabet in relief.

Located on the perimeter of the Expo site, the pavilion takes advantage of views towards the Huangpu River and the Shanghai skyline in the distance.

Inside the pavilion

Signs become spaces while
spaces become signs.

Sequential lighting is programmed to highlight
individual Hangeul Pixels at night.

shanghai corporate.

Atelier Feichang Jianzhu.

A dense infrastructural matrix envelops a collection of irregularly shaped spaces, unifying diverse programs and volumes into a rectangular block. This is a recurrent compositional strategy at the Expo and a compelling model for urban buildings in general. It is a way to transition from increasingly complex programs and interior configurations to a consolidated mass and iconic presence on the street.

The building pays homage to the groundbreaking Centre Georges Pompidou of 1976 with its exposed infrastructure and ductwork. In lieu of massive structural members and conduits the Corporate Pavilion presents a filigree of infrastructure. While the Centre Georges Pompidou flaunted technology in the form of colossal machinery this pavilion appeals to a different technological paradigm: information technology and miniaturization.

The building is enveloped in a mist of technology: a cloud-like distribution of miniaturized structure, electronics and digital bits. This steel and silicon filigree features arrays of sensors and actuators that enable the building envelope to respond to ambient conditions and accordingly enhance its environmental performance. Embedded misters, for instance, produce an actual cloud of cooling vapor that regulates the ambient temperature. This climate-control device responsively boosts the environmental performance of the building while visually enhancing the foamy character of the façade.

Embedded LEDs transform the building into an active digital display controlled by computers that alter the appearance of the building in a variety of automated or programmed ways, further underscoring the shift from the iconography of the machine to the atmospherics of the information age.

ing Materials,

Interior spaces

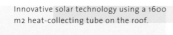

Innovative solar technology using a 1600 m2 heat-collecting tube on the roof.

The infrastructure is designated for a variety
of environmental functions including solar
energy harvesting and rain water collection.

LEDs and misters change the appearance of
the building in response to environmental
conditions or computerized programs.

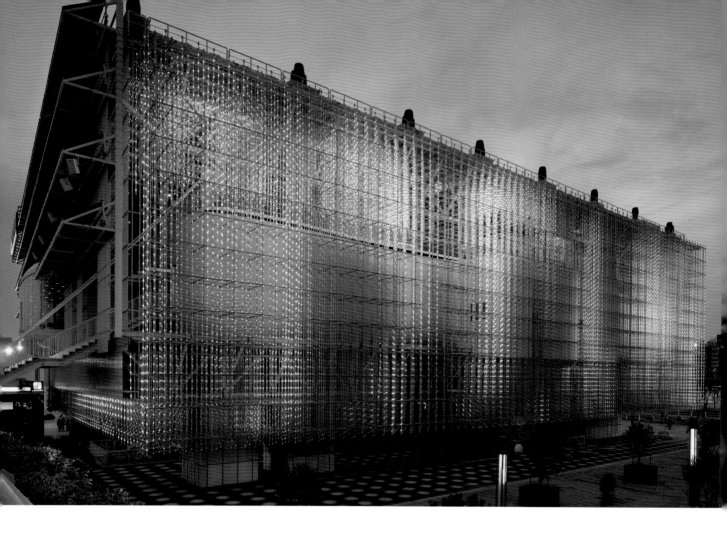

The Shanghai Corporate Pavilion is encased
in a dense infrastructural meshwork.

Retail area

Interior spaces

The Shanghai Corporate Pavilion features colored LEDs that transform the building at night.

Multicolored tube matrix and LEDs transform the
building inside and out

Auditorium and exhibition spaces

Inside the exhibition space

The tube matrix and LED
lighting system

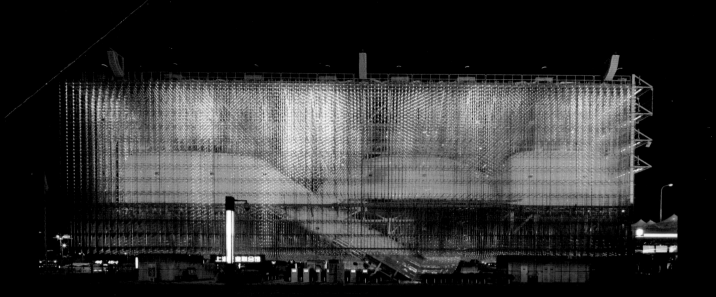

The LEDs are computer-controlled
for swiftly coordinated effects.

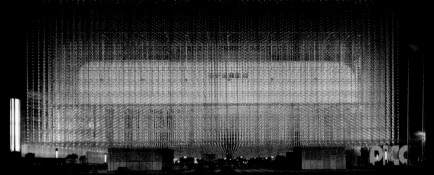

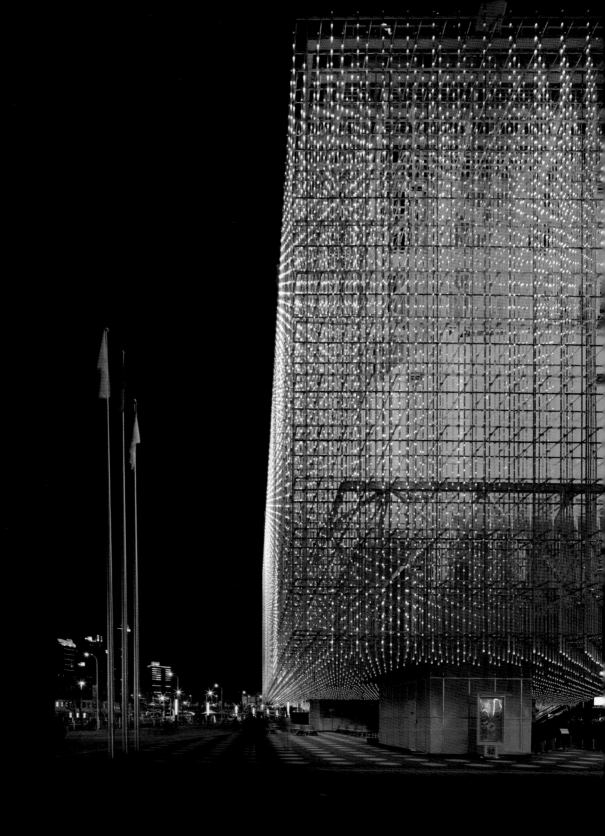

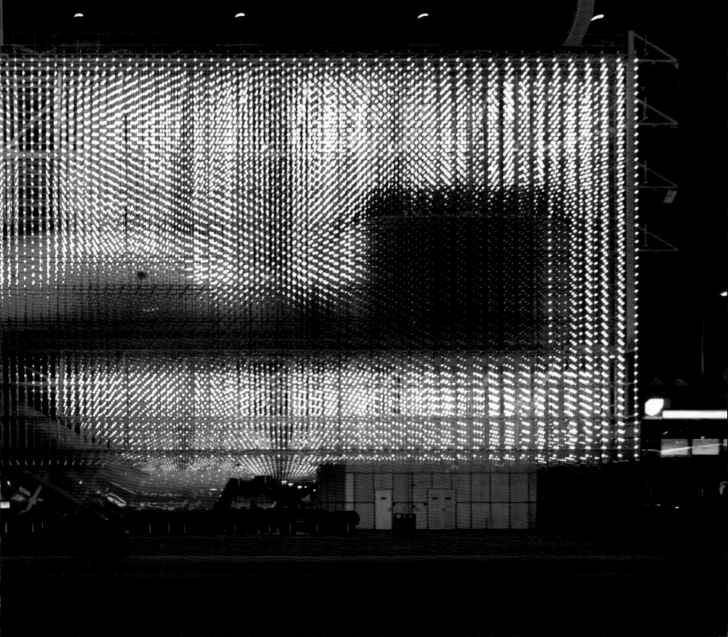

EXPO AXIS

Architects
SBA design Stuttgart/Shanghai

Theme
*Main entrance and central traffic
landscape line at the Expo site*

Buliding Area
130,000 square meters

Total Floor Area
250,000 square meters

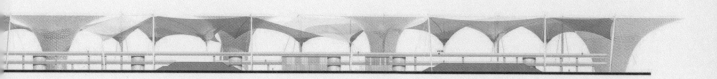

ELEVATION EAST 1:500

ELEVATION WEST 1:500

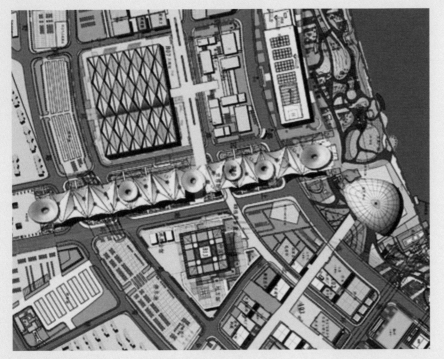

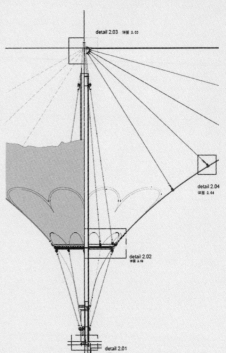

detail 2.03 详图 2.03

detail 2.04 详图 2.04

detail 2.02 详图 2.02

detail 2.01 详图 2.01

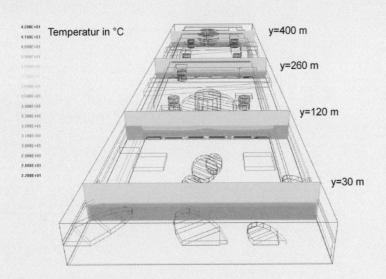

Temperatur in °C

4.200E+01
4.100E+01
4.000E+01
3.900E+01
3.800E+01
3.700E+01
3.600E+01
3.500E+01
3.400E+01
3.300E+01
3.200E+01
3.100E+01
3.000E+01
2.900E+01
2.800E+01
2.700E+01

y=400 m

y=260 m

y=120 m

y=30 m

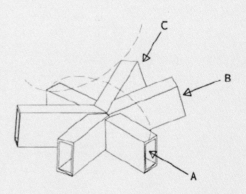

C

B

A

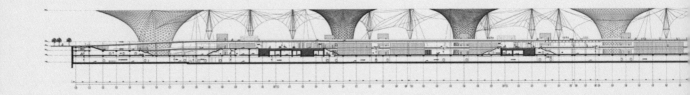

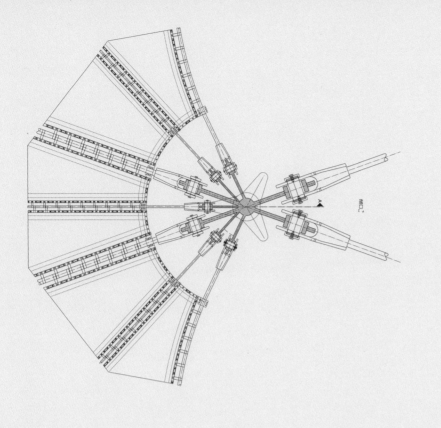

section A-A   section B-B   section C-C

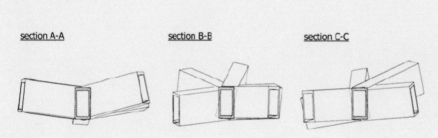

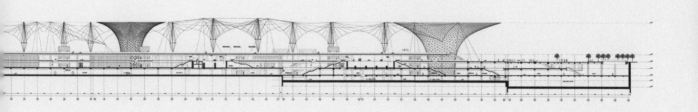

CHILE PAVILION

Architects
Sabbagh Arquitectos

Theme
City of Relations

Area
3,000 square meters

Location
Zone C, Expo Site

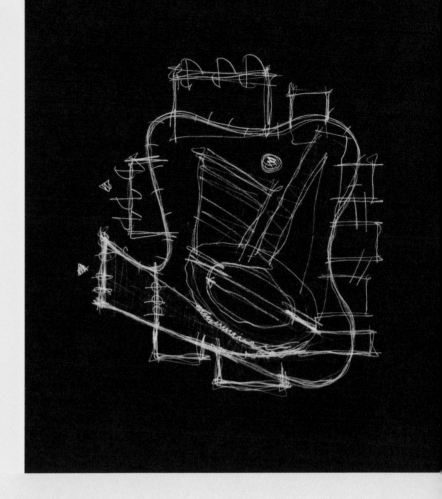

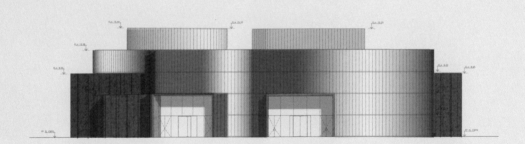

WEST ELEVATION

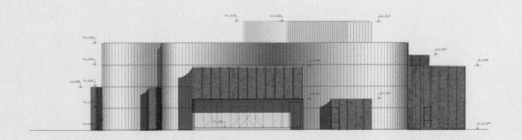

SOUTH ELEVATION

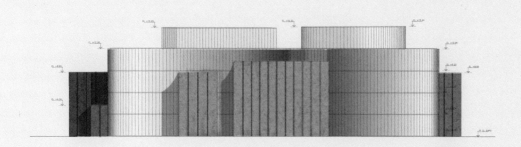

EAST ELEVATION
SCALE 1:100

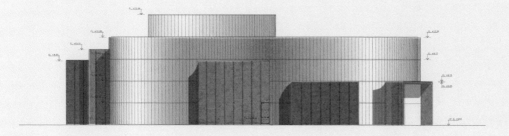

NORTH ELEVATION
SCALE 1:100

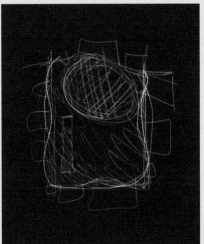
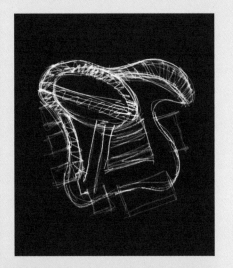

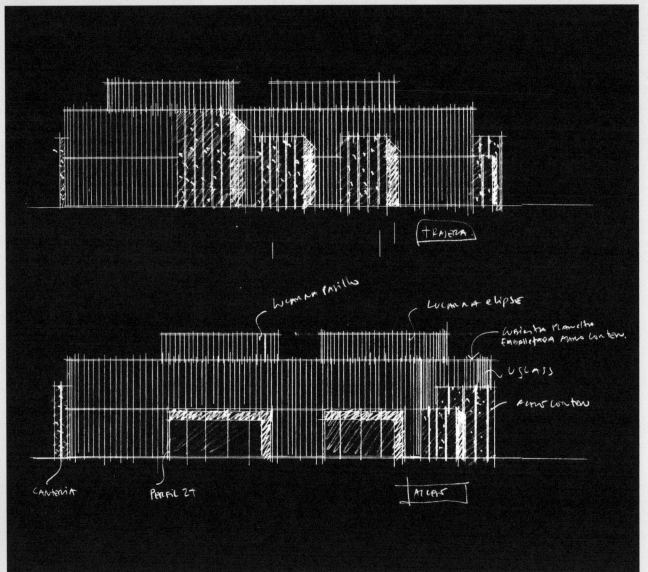

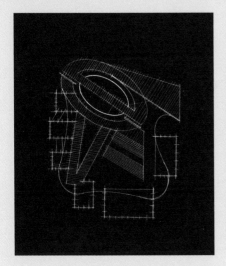
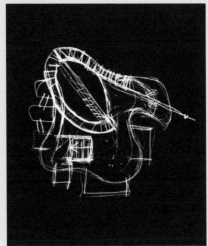
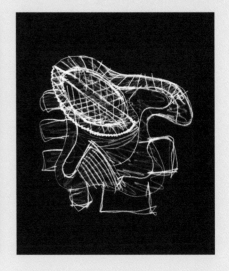

GENERAL PLAN   ESCALA 1 : 1000

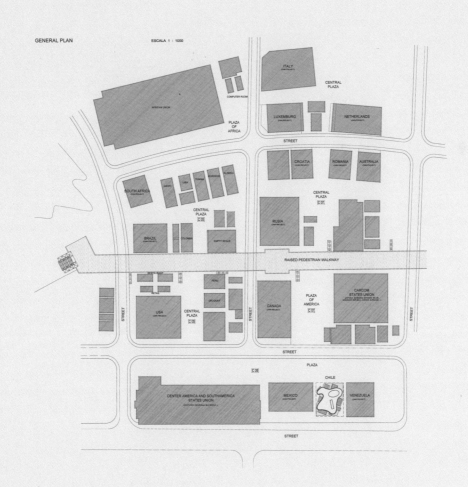

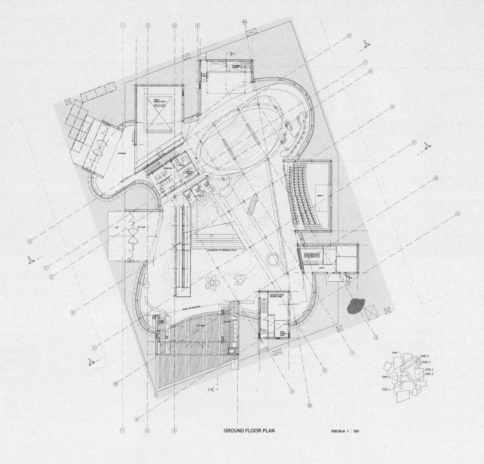

GROUND FLOOR PLAN   ESCALA 1 : 100

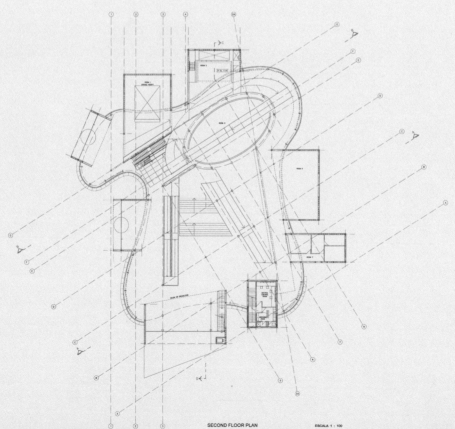

SECOND FLOOR PLAN   ESCALA 1 : 100

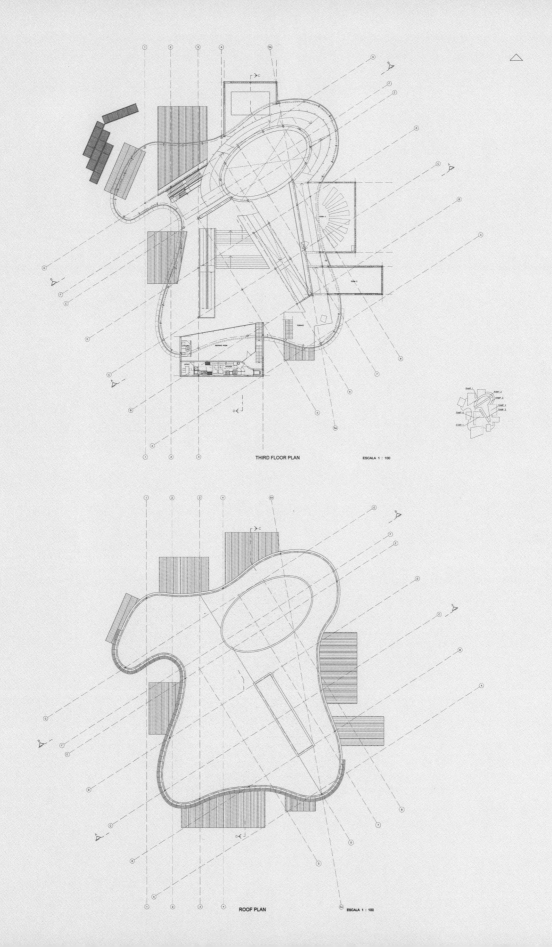

THIRD FLOOR PLAN   ESCALA 1 : 100

ROOF PLAN   ESCALA 1 : 100

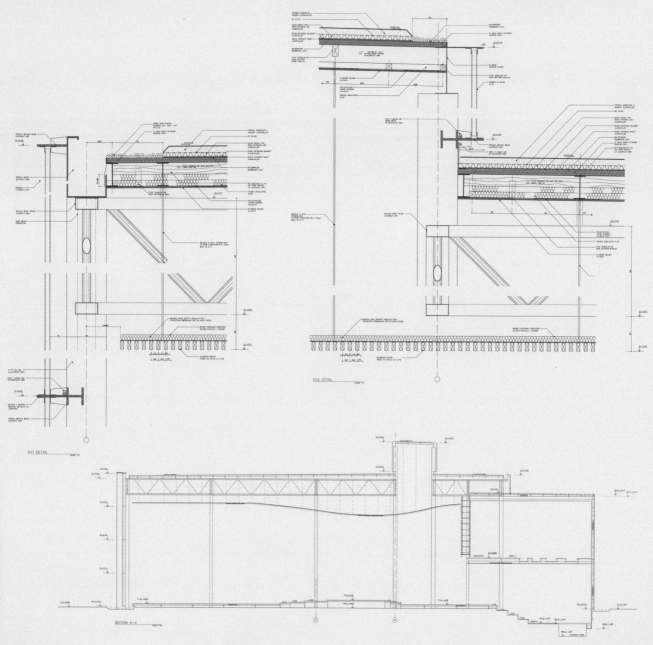

DV1 DETAIL

DV2 DETAIL

SECTION A-A

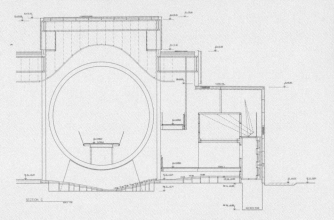

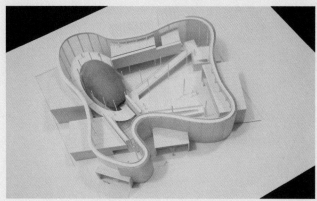

SECTION C

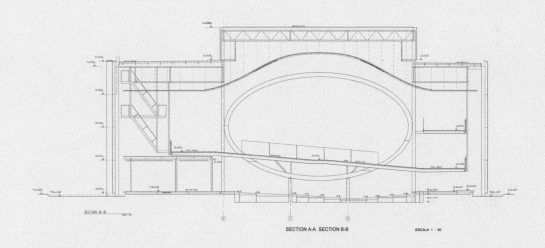

SECTION B-B

SECTION A-A SECTION B-B   ESCALA 1 : 50

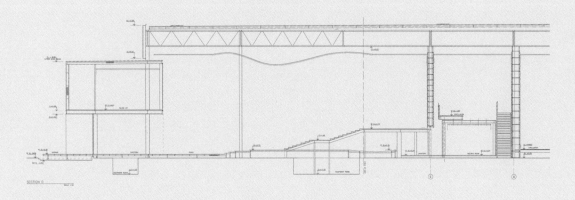

SECTION D

SECTION C-C SECTION D-D   ESCALA 1 : 50

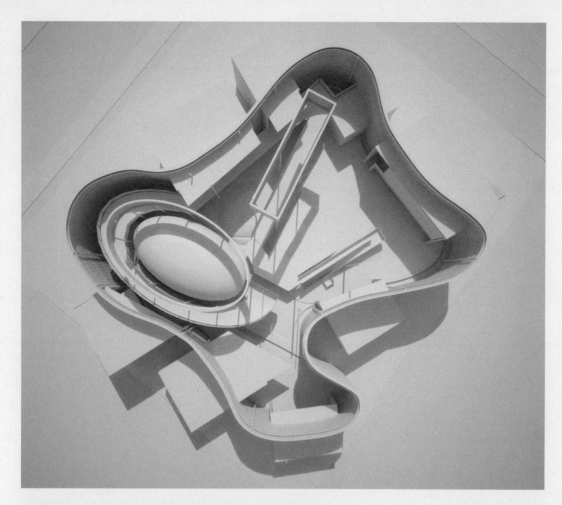

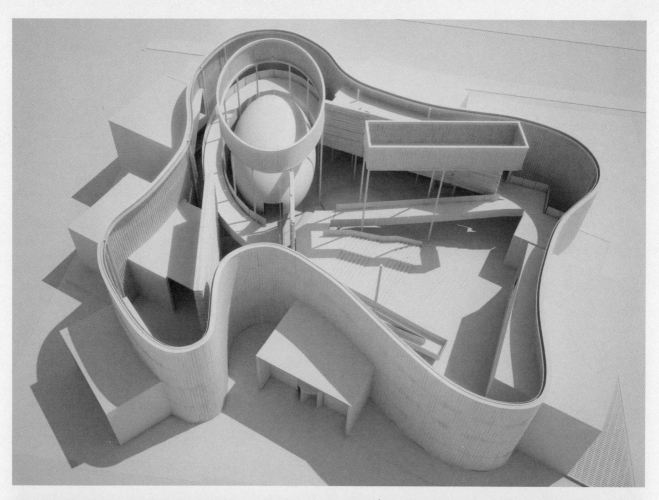

SPAIN PAVILION

Architects
Benedetta Tagliabue

Theme
*From the City of Our Parents to
the City of Our Children*

Area
6,000 square meters

Location
Zone C, Expo Site

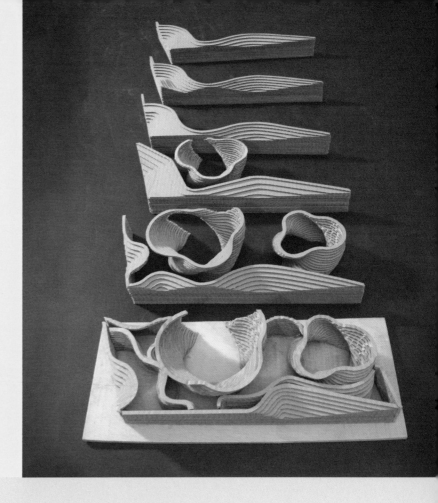

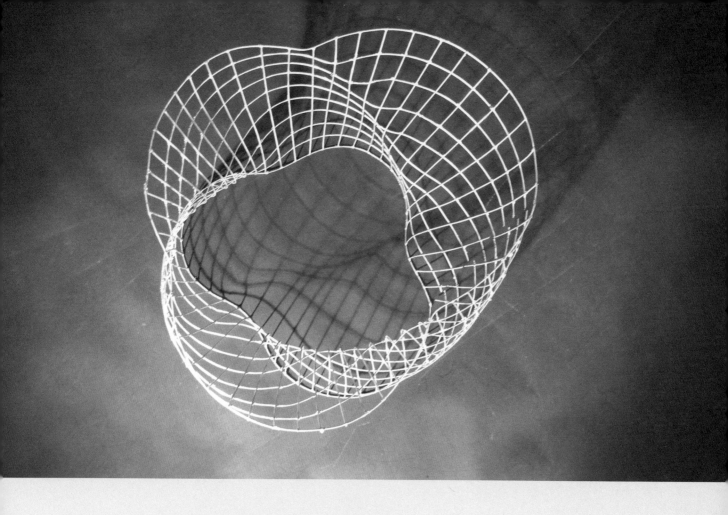

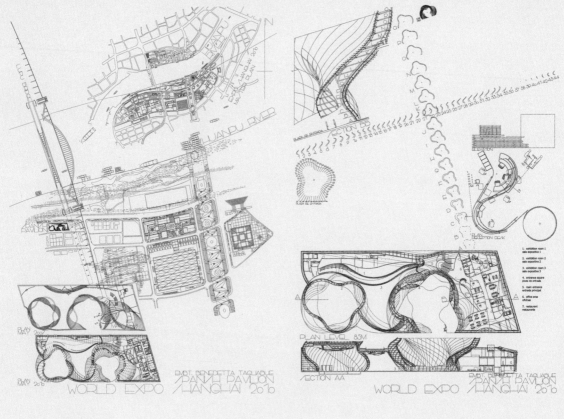

SECTION BB

PLAN LEVEL 8.5M

SECTION AA

1 exhibition room 1
sala expositiva 1
2 exhibition room 2
sala expositiva 2
3 exhibition room 3
sala expositiva 3
4 entrance square
plaza de entrada
5 main entrance
entrada principal
6 office area
oficinas
7 restaurant
restaurante

EMBT. BENEDETTA TAGLIABUE
SPAIN PAVILION
WORLD EXPO SHANGHAI 2010

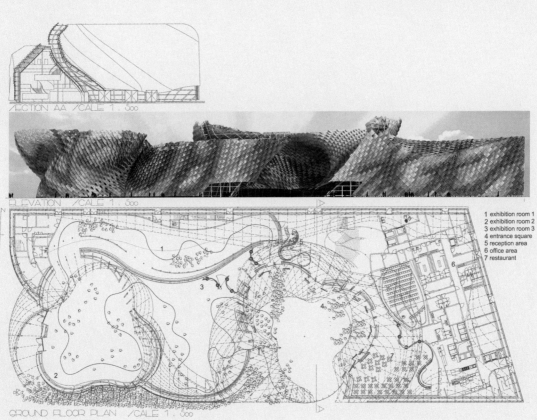

SECTION AA SCALE 1:500

ELEVATION SCALE 1:500

GROUND FLOOR PLAN SCALE 1:500

1 exhibition room 1
2 exhibition room 2
3 exhibition room 3
4 entrance square
5 reception area
6 office area
7 restaurant

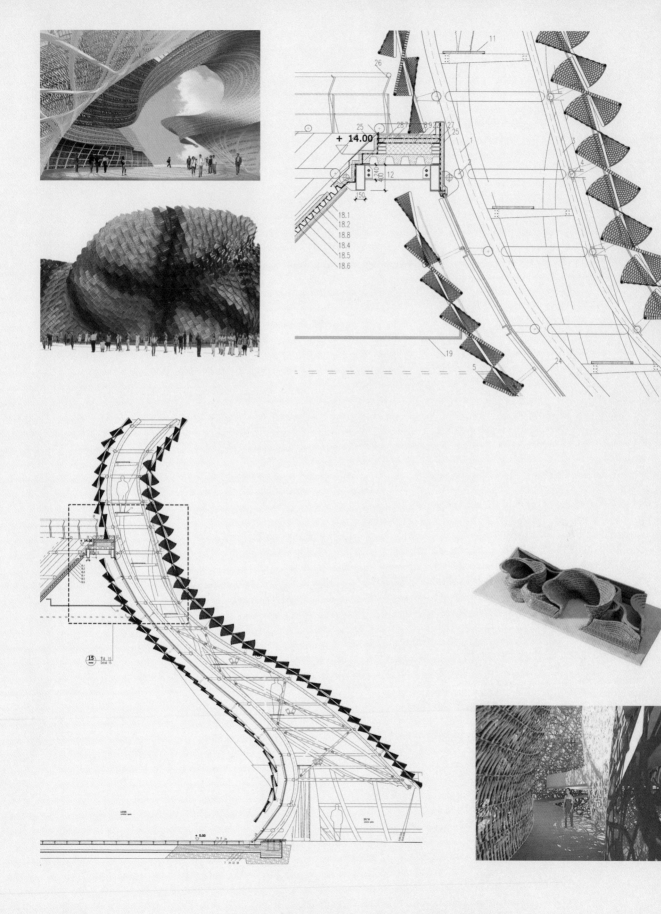

TIPOS DE PANELES
TYPES OF PANEL

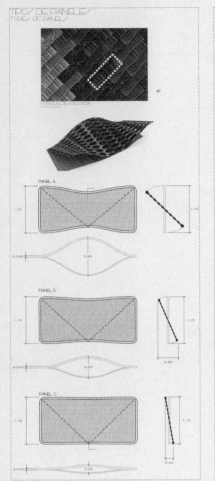

PANEL A

PANEL B

PANEL C

TRENZADO Y COLORES
WEAVE AND COLORS

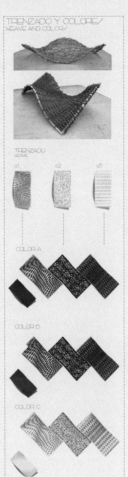

TRENZADO
WEAVE

COLOR A

COLOR B

COLOR C

SISTEMA DE ANCLAJE DE PANELES

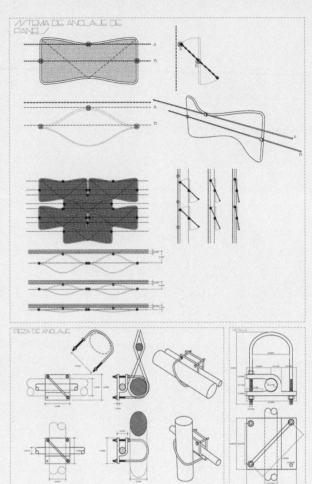

PIEZA DE ANCLAJE

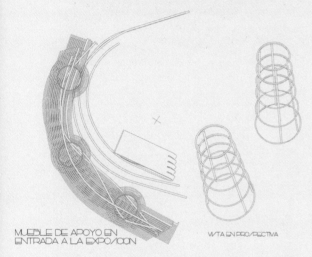

MUEBLE DE APOYO EN
ENTRADA A LA EXPOSICION

VISTA EN PROSPECTIVA

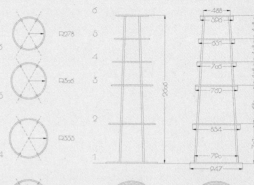

R278

R306

R333

R361

R467

Ø 3MM
Ø 2MM
R433

MATERIALES
ACERO PINTADO DE BLANCO

PABELLON DE ESPANA
EXPO SHANGHAI 2010

UBICACION   SHANGHAI

ARQUITECTO   MIRALLES TAGLIABUE - EMBT
              Benedetta Tagliabue   Barcelona 08002
              Passatge de la Pau,   T +34 93 412 53 42
              10 bis, pral.   info@mirallestagliabue.com

CLIENTE   SEEI
              Sociedad Estatal
              Exposiciones   C/Cea de José Abascal,4
              Internacionales, SLA 28003, Madrid

FECHA   MARZO 2009

ESCALA   1/6

MUEBLE DE APOYO EN
ENTRADA

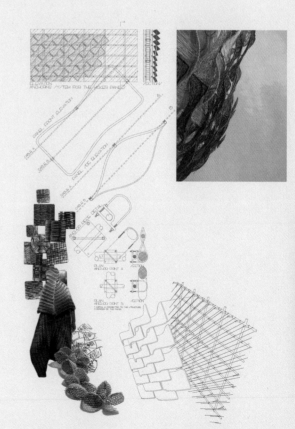

FRANCE PAVILION

Architects
Jacques Ferrier Architectures

Theme
The Sensual City

Area
6,000 square meters

Location
Zone C, Expo Site

france.

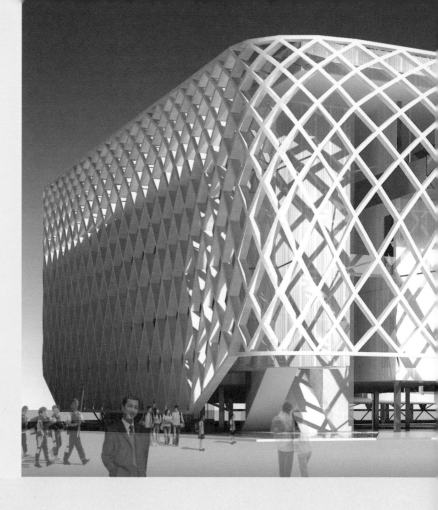

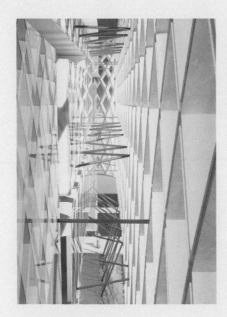

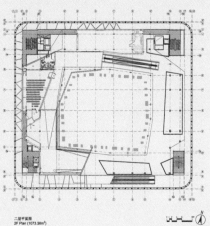

一层平面图
1F Plan (803.67m²)

二层平面图
2F Plan (1073.36m²)

三层平面图
3F Plan (2199.26m²)

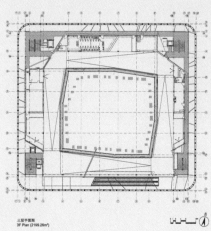

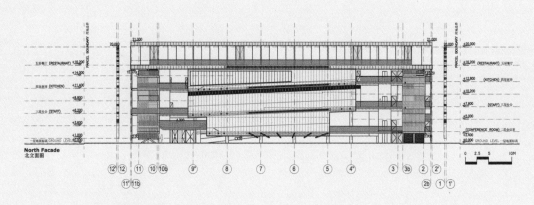

五层餐厅 (RESTAURANT) +18,200
+14,000
四层厨房 (KITCHEN) +11,400
+8,800
三层办公 (STAFF) +6,200
+3,800
一层地面标高 GROUND LEVEL +1,000
±0,000

PARCEL BOUNDARY 用地边界线

20,000

PARCEL BOUNDARY 用地边界线

21,000 +21,000

+18,200 (RESTAURANT) 五层餐厅
+14,000
+12,800 (KITCHEN) 四层厨房
+10,200
+7,000 (STAFF) 三层办公
+5,000
(CONFERENCE ROOM) 二层会议室 +2,400
±0,000 GROUND LEVEL 一层地面标高

North Facade
北立面图

0 2.5 5   10M

⑫' ⑫ ⑪ ⑩ ⑩b ⑨" ⑧ ⑦ ⑥ ⑤ ④" ③ ③b ② ②'
⑪" ⑪b   ②b ① ①'

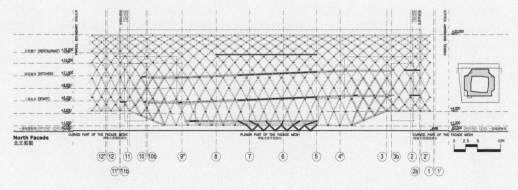

五层餐厅 (RESTAURANT) +18,200
+14,000
四层厨房 (KITCHEN) +11,400
+8,800
三层办公 (STAFF) +6,200
+3,800
一层地面标高 GROUND LEVEL +1,000
±0,000

PARCEL BOUNDARY 用地边界线

+20,000

PARCEL BOUNDARY 用地边界线

+4,000

+1,000
±0,000 GROUND LEVEL 一层地面标高

North Facade
北立面图

CURVED PART OF THE FACADE MESH
网格立面曲面部分

PLANAR PART OF THE FACADE MESH
网格立面平面部分

CURVED PART OF THE FACADE MESH
网格立面曲面部分

0 2.5 5   10M

⑫' ⑫ ⑪ ⑩ ⑩b ⑨" ⑧ ⑦ ⑥ ⑤ ④" ③ ③b ② ②'
⑪" ⑪b   ②b ① ①'

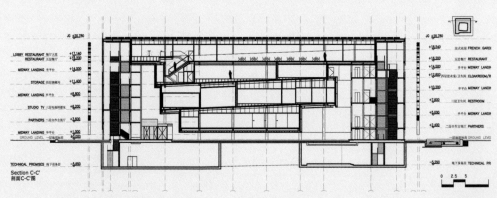

JG +20,280   JG +20,280

LOBBY RESTAURANT 餐厅大堂 +17,140
RESTAURANT 五层餐厅 +8,500
MIDWAY LANDING 半平台 +14,000
STORAGE 四层储藏间 +11,400
MIDWAY LANDING 半平台 +8,800
STUDIO TV 三层电视拍摄室 +6,200
PARTNERS 二层合作方展厅 +3,800
MIDWAY LANDING 半平台 +1,000
GROUND LEVEL 一层地面标高 ±0,000

法式花园 FRENCH GARD
+18,140
五层餐厅 RESTAURANT +18,200
平台 MIDWAY LAND
+12,800 四层衣帽间/卫生间 CLOAKROOM/R
平台 MIDWAY LAND
+10,200
三层卫生间 RESTROOM +7,800
半平台 MIDWAY LAND
+5,000
二层合作方展厅 PARTNERS +2,400
一层地面标高 GROUND LEVE

TECHNICAL PREMISES 地下设备层 -5,650

-5,280 地下设备层 TECHNICAL PR

Section C-C'
剖面C-C'图

0 2.5 5

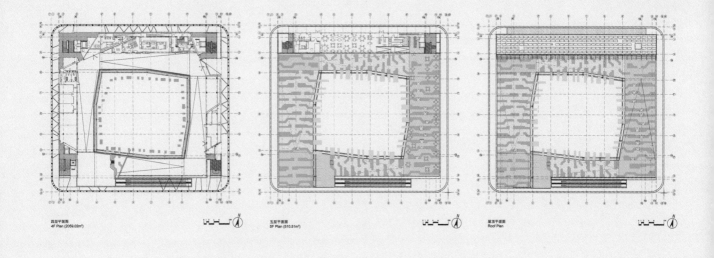

四层平面图 (2059.02m²)
4F Plan (2059.02m²)

五层平面图 (510.51m²)
5F Plan (510.51m²)

屋顶平面图
Roof Plan

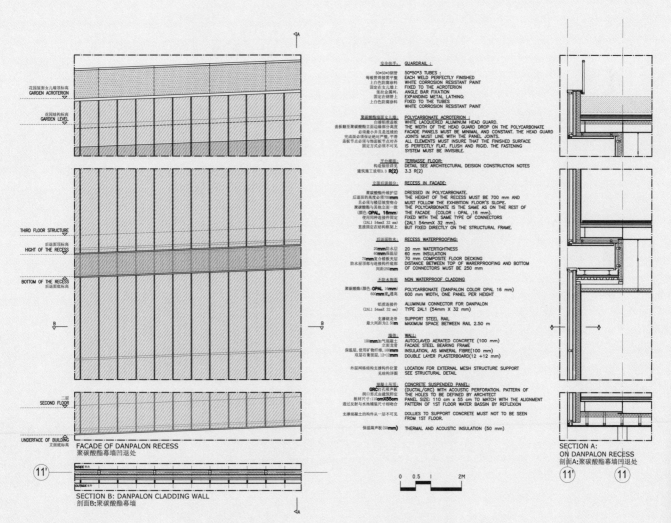

花园屋面女儿墙顶标高
GARDEN ACROTERION

花园结构标高
GARDEN LEVEL

THIRD FLOOR STRUCTURE

后退面顶部标高
HIGHT OF THE RECESS

后退面底标高
BOTTOM OF THE RECESS

SECOND FLOOR

UNDERFACE OF BUILDING
立面底标高

FACADE OF DANPALON RECESS
聚碳酸酯幕墙凹退处

SECTION B: DANPALON CLADDING WALL
剖面B:聚碳酸酯幕墙

INSIDE 内侧
OUTSIDE 外侧

安全扶手: **GUARDRAIL :**
50*50*3钢管 | 50*50*3 TUBES :
每根管焊接剪平整 | EACH WELD PERFECTLY FINISHED
上白色防腐涂料 | WHITE CORROSION RESISTANT PAINT
固定在女儿墙上 | FIXED TO THE ACROTERION
张拉金属网, | ANGLE BAR FIXATION
固定在钢管上 | EXPANDING METAL LATHING:
上白色防腐涂料 | FIXED TO THE TUBES
| WHITE CORROSION RESISTANT PAINT

聚碳酸酯墙面女儿墙: **POLYCARBONATE ACROTERION :**
白漆铝盖压板 | WHITE LACQUERED ALUMINUM HEAD GUARD.
盖板翻至聚碳酸酯立面边缘部分高度 | THE WIDTH OF THE HEAD GUARD DROP ON THE POLYCARBONATE
必须最小并且连续性 | FACADE PANELS MUST BE MINIMAL AND CONSTANT. THE HEAD GUARD
完成面必须促进绝对平整、平滑 | JOINTS MUST LINE WITH THE PANEL JOINTS.
盖板节点必须与墙面板节点对齐 | ALL ELEMENTS MUST INSURE THAT THE FINISHED SURFACE
固定方式必须可见 | IS PERFECTLY FLAT, FLUSH AND RIGID. THE FASTENING
| SYSTEM MUST BE INVISIBLE.

平台楼面: **TERRASSE FLOOR:**
构造做法详见 **R(2)** | DETAIL SEE ARCHITECTURAL DEISIGN CONSTRUCTION NOTES
建筑施工设明3.3 **R(2)** | 3.3 R(2)

立面后退部分: **RECESS IN FACADE:**
聚碳酸酯外侧护层 | DRESSED IN POLYCARBONATE.
后退面的高度必须700mm | THE HEIGHT OF THE RECESS MUST BE 700 mm AND
且必须与楼层坡度吻合 | MUST FOLLOW THE EXHIBITION FLOOR'S SLOPE.
聚碳酸酯与其他立面一致 | THE POLYCARBONATE IS THE SAME AS ON THE REST OF
(颜色 **OPAL, 16mm**) | THE FACADE (COLOR : OPAL , 16 mm).
使用同种连接件固定 | FIXED WITH THE SAME TYPE OF CONNECTORS
(2AL1 54mmX 32 mm) | (2AL1 54mmX 32 mm).
直接固定于结构板架上 | BUT FIXED DIRECTLY ON THE STRUCTURAL FRAME.

后退面防水: **RECESS WATERPROOFING:**
20mm防水层 | 20 mm WATERTIGHTNESS
60mm保温层 | 60 mm INSULATION
70mm复合楼板完成 | 70 mm COMPOSITE FLOOR DECKING
防水层顶部与连接件距离 | DISTANCE BETWEEN TOP OF WARERPROOFING AND BOTTOM
间距250mm | OF CONNECTORS MUST BE 250 mm

不防水饰面: **NON WATERPROOF CLADDING**
聚碳酸酯(颜色 **OPAL** 16mm) | POLYCARBONATE (DANPALON COLOR OPAL 16 mm)
600mm宽度,层高 | 600 mm WIDTH, ONE PANEL PER HEIGHT

铝质连接件 | ALUMINUM CONNECTOR FOR DANPALON
(2AL1 54mmX 32 mm) | TYPE 2AL1 (54mm X 32 mm)

支撑钢龙骨 | SUPPORT STEEL RAIL
最大间距为2.50m | MAXIMUM SPACE BETWEEN RAIL 2.50 m

墙体: **WALL:**
100mm加气混凝土 | AUTOCLAVED AERATED CONCRETE (100 mm)
立面支撑 | FACADE STEEL BEARING FRAME
保温层,使用矿物纤维(100mm) | INSULATION, AS MINERAL FIBRE(100 mm)
双层石膏板(12+12mm) | DOUBLE LAYER PLASTERBOARD(12 +12 mm)

外层网格结构支撑件位置 | LOCATION FOR EXTERNAL MESH STRUCTURE SUPPORT
见结构详图 | SEE STRUCTURAL DETAIL

混凝土吊顶: **CONCRETE SUSPENDED PANEL:**
GRC带孔吸声板 | (DUCTAL/GRC) WITH ACOUSTIC PERFORATION. PATTERN OF
开口型式由建筑师定 | THE HOLES TO BE DEFINED BY ARCHITECT
板材尺寸:110**cmX55cm** | PANEL SIZE: 110 cm x 55 cm TO MATCH WITH THE ALIGNMENT
通过反射与水池铺做尺寸相吻合 | PATTERN OF 1ST FLOOR WATER BASSIN BY REFLEXION

支撑混凝土的件从一层不可见 | DOLLIES TO SUPPORT CONCRETE MUST NOT TO BE SEEN
| FROM 1ST FLOOR.

保温隔声板(50mm) | THERMAL AND ACOUSTIC INSULATION (50 mm)

0 0.5 1   2M

SECTION A:
ON DANPALON RECESS
剖面A:聚碳酸酯幕墙凹退处

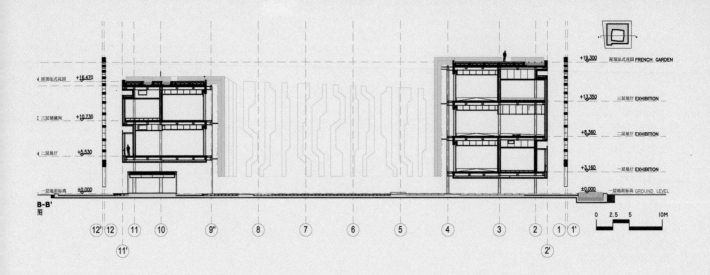

294

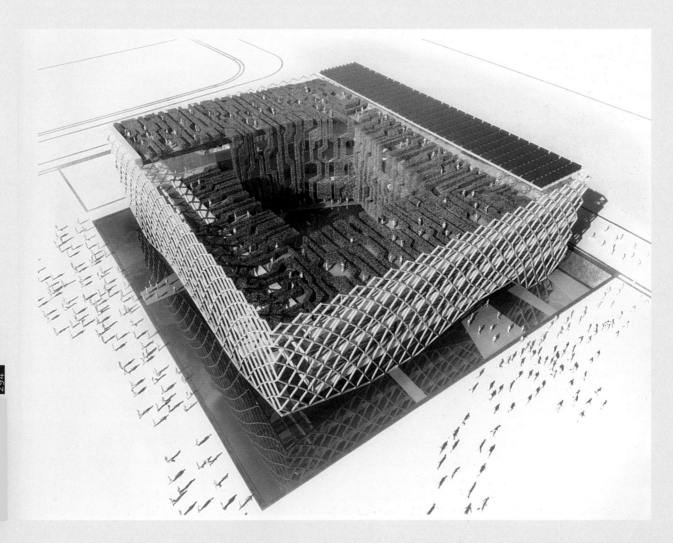

HISTORY SKETCHES MODELS 3D MODELS PROTOTYPES ON SITE

THE **VERTICAL GARDEN**

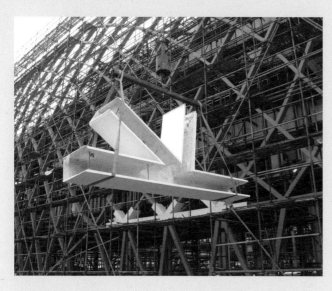

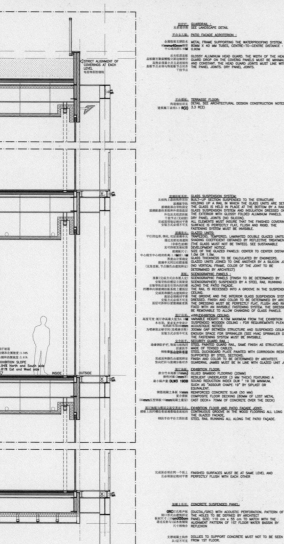

GUARDRAIL :
SEE LANDSCAPE DETAIL

PATIO FAÇADE ACROTERION :
METAL FRAME SUPPORTING THE WATERPROOFING SYSTEM.
80MM X 40 MM TUBES, CENTRE-TO-CENTRE DISTANCE :
0.90M

GLOSSY ALUMINUM HEAD GUARD. THE WIDTH OF THE HEAD
GUARD DROP ON THE COVERING PANELS MUST BE MINIMAL
AND CONSTANT. THE HEAD GUARD JOINTS MUST LINE WITH
THE PANEL JOINTS. DRY PANEL JOINTS.

TERRASSE FLOOR:
DETAIL SEE ARCHITECTURAL DESIGN CONSTRUCTION NOTES
3.3 R(2)

GLASS SUSPENSION SYSTEM:
BUILT-UP SECTION SUSPENDED TO THE STRUCTURE
HOLDING UP A RAIL IN WHICH THE GLASS UNITS ARE SET.
THE GLASS IS HELD IN PLACE AT THE BOTTOM BY A RAIL.
GLASS SUSPENSION SYSTEM AND INSULATION DRESSED ON
THE EXTERIOR WITH GLOSSY FOLDED ALUMINUM PANELS.
DRY PANEL JOINTS (NO SILICON).
ALL ELEMENTS MUST INSURE THAT THE FINISHED COVERING
SURFACE IS PERFECTLY FLAT, FLUSH AND RIGID. THE
FASTENING SYSTEM MUST BE INVISIBLE.

GLAZED UNITS:
TRAPEZOID, TEMPERED, LAMINATED DOUBLE GLAZED UNITS.
SHADING COEFFICIENT OBTAINED BY REFLECTIVE TREATMENT
(THE GLASS MUST NOT BE TINTED). SEE SUSTAINABLE
DEVELOPMENT NOTICE.
SIZE OF THE GLAZED PANELS: CENTER TO CENTER DISTANCE :
1.0M OR 1.5M.
GLASS THICKNESS TO BE CALCULATED BY ENGINEERS.
GLAZED UNITS JOINED TO ONE ANOTHER BY A SILICON JOINT
(NO VERTICAL FRAME). COLOR OF THE JOINT TO BE
DETERMINED BY ARCHITECT)

SCENOGRAPHIC PANELS :
SCENOGRAPHIC PANELS (FINISH TO BE DETERMINED BY
SCENOGRAPHER) SUSPENDED BY A STEEL RAIL RUNNING ALL
ALONG THE PATIO FAÇADE.
THE RAIL IS RECESSED INTO A GROOVE IN THE SUSPENDED
CEILING.
THE GROOVE AND THE INTERIOR GLASS SUSPENSION SYSTEM ARE
DRESSED. FINISH AND COLOR TO BE DETERMINED BY ARCHITECT.
THE DRESSING MUST BE PERFECTLY FLAT, FLUSH AND RIGID AND
FIXED WITH AN INVISIBLE FASTENING SYSTEM. THE DRESSING MUST
BE REMOVABLE TO ALLOW CHANGING OF GLASS PANELS.

EXHIBITION CEILING:
VARIABLE HEIGHT: 4.10M MAXIMUM FROM THE EXHIBITION FLOOR.
SUSPENDED WOODEN CEILING : FOR REQUIREMENTS PLEASE SEE
ACOUSTIQUE NOTICE
300MM GAP BETWEEN STRUCTURE AND SUSPENDED CEILING TO LEAVE
ENOUGH SPACE FOR SPRINKLER (SEE HVAC SPRINKLER DETAIL)
THE FASTENING SYSTEM MUST BE INVISIBLE.

SECURITY GUARD RAIL:
STEEL PAINTED GUARD RAIL, SAME FINISH AS STRUCTURE. HAND RAILS
MADE OF TENSED CABLES.
STEEL DUCKBOARD PLATE PAINTED WITH CORROSION RESISTANT PAINT,
SUPPORTED BY STEEL SECTIONS.
FINISH AND COLOR TO BE DETERMINED BY ARCHITECT.
GUARDRAIL JAMBS MUST BE IN LINE WITH GLAZED UNIT JOINTS.

EXHIBITION FLOOR:
GLUED BAMBOO FLOORING (20MM)
RESILIENT UNDERLAYER (3 MM THICK) FEATURING A
SOUND REDUCTION INDEX DLW `19 DB MINIMUM,
SUCH AS "ASSOUR CHAPE " BY SIPLAST OR
EQUIVALENT.
REINFORCED CONCRETE SLAB (50 MM)
COMPOSITE FLOOR DECKING (60MM OF LOST METAL
CAST DECK+ 70MM OF CONCRETE OVER THE DECK)

EXHIBITION FLOOR AND PATIO JOINT:
CONTINUOUS GROOVE IN THE WOOD FLOORING ALL LONG
THE GLAZED FAÇADE.
STEEL RAIL RUNNING ALL ALONG THE PATIO FAÇADE.

FINISHED SURFACES MUST BE AT SAME LEVEL AND
PERFECTLY FLUSH WITH EACH OTHER

CONCRETE SUSPENDED PANEL:
(DUCTAL/GRC) WITH ACOUSTIC PERFORATION, PATTERN OF
THE HOLES TO BE DEFINED BY ARCHITECT
PANEL SIZE: 110 cm x 55 cm TO MATCH WITH THE
ALIGNMENT PATTERN OF 1ST FLOOR WATER BASSIN BY
REFLEXION

DOLLIES TO SUPPORT CONCRETE MUST NOT TO BE SEEN
FROM 1ST FLOOR.

THERMAL AND ACOUSTIC INSULATION (50 mm)

STRICT ALIGNMENT OF
COVERINGS AT EACH
LEVEL

EXHIBITION SLOPE
3.04% North and South side
3.81% East and West side

INSIDE   OUTSIDE

GLAZED FACADE SECTION
玻璃幕墙剖面

0   0.5   1

9"

UNITED KINGDOM PAVILION

Architects
Heatherwick Studio

Theme
*Building on the Past,
Shaping our Future*

Area
6,000 square meters

Location
Zone D, Expo Site

uk.

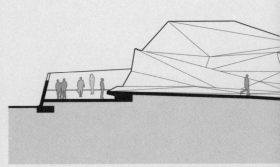

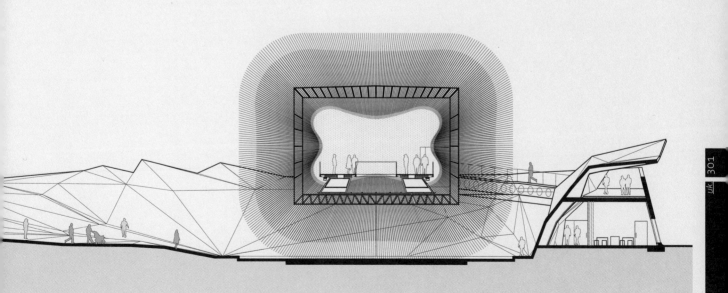

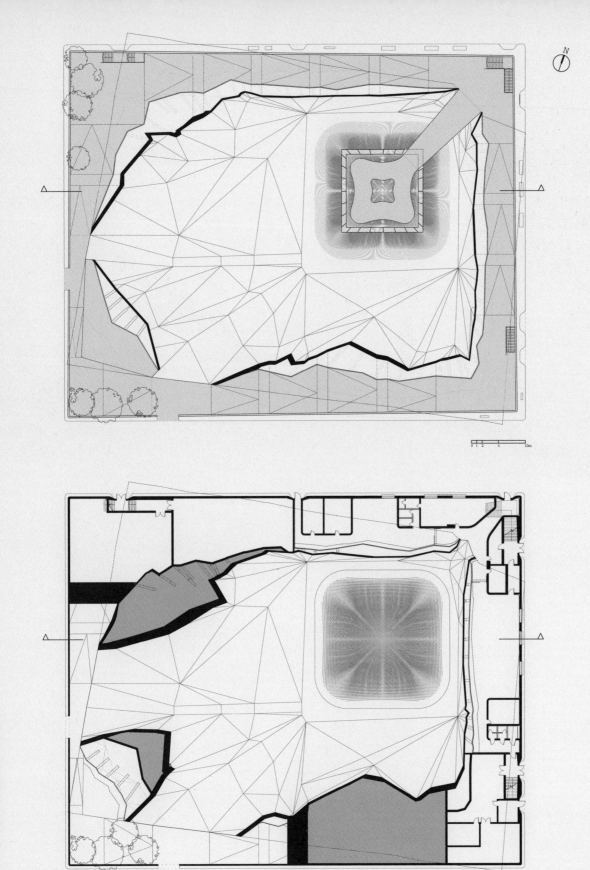

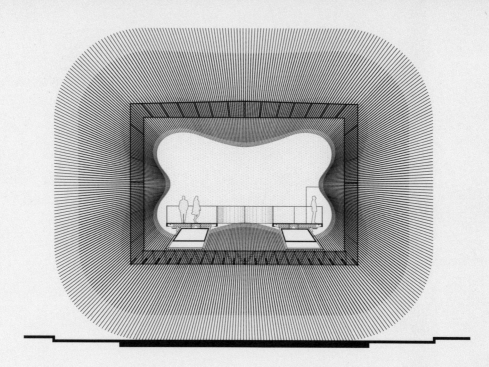

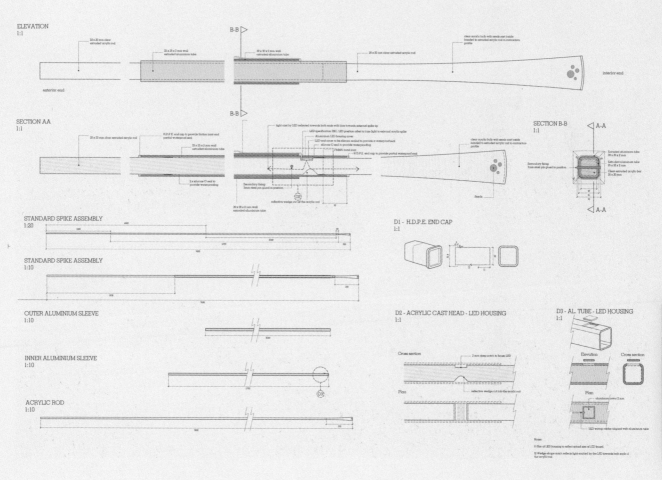

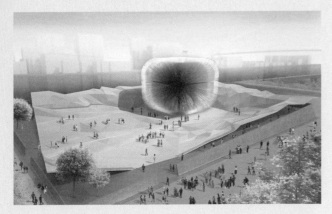

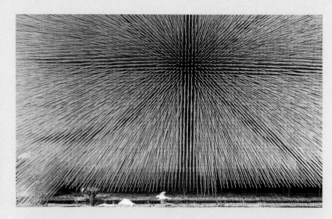

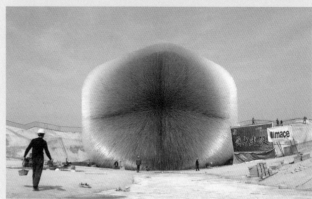

FINLAND PAVILION

Architects
JKMM Architects

Theme
*Well Being, Competence
and Environment*

Area
3,000 square meters

Location
Zone C, Expo Site

finland.

冰壶 KISNU

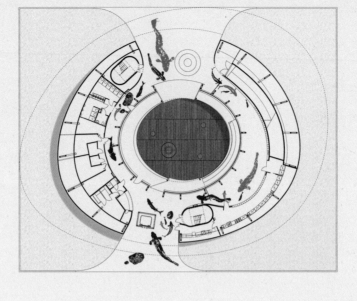

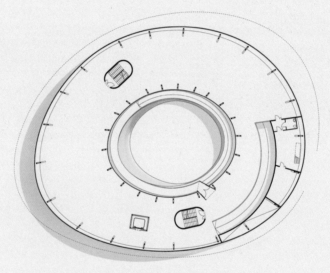

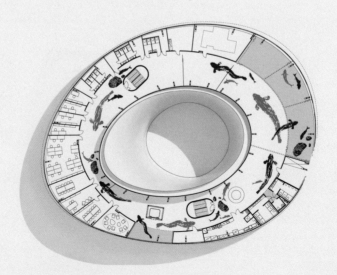

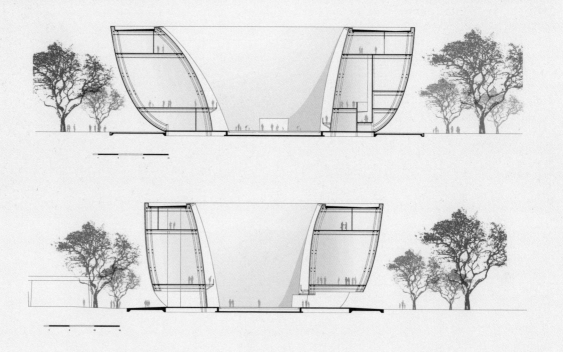

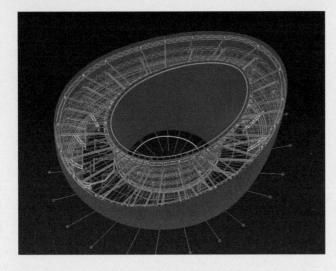

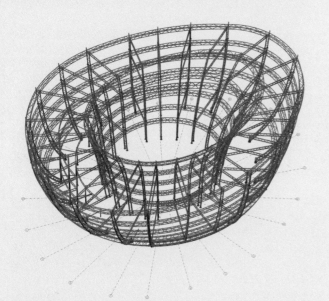

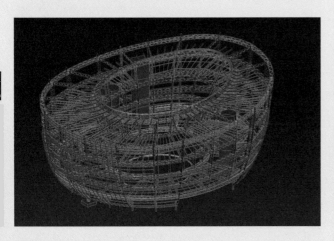
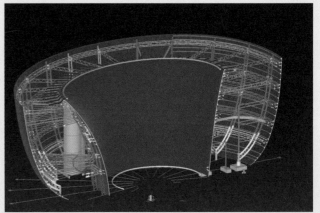

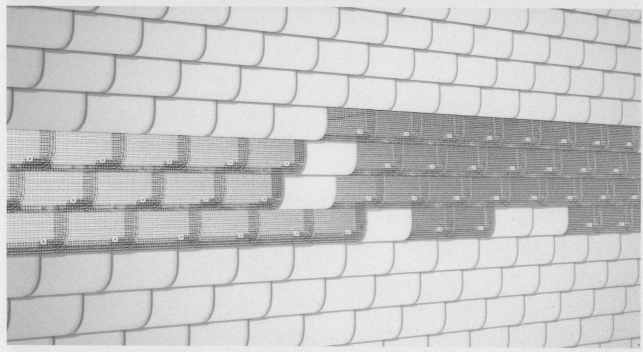

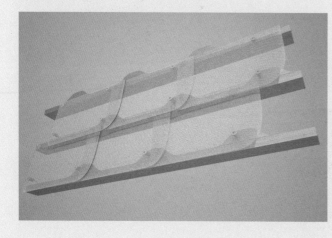

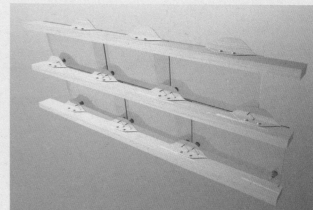

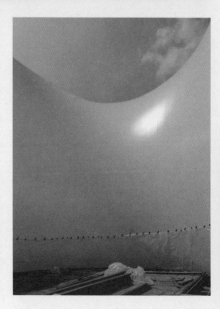

DENMARK PAVILION

Architects
Big Architects

Theme
Wellfairytales

Area
3,000 square meters

Location
Zone C, Expo Site

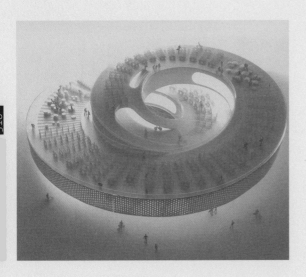

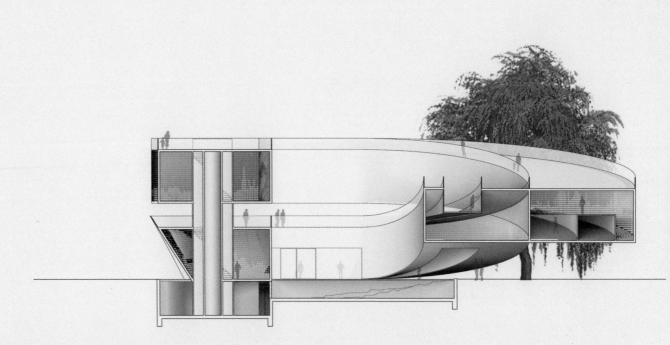

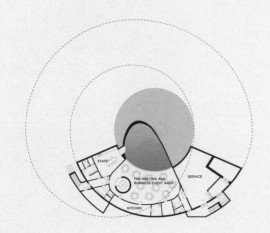

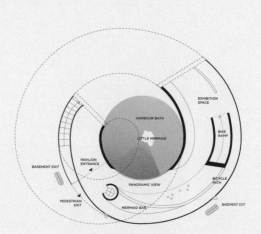

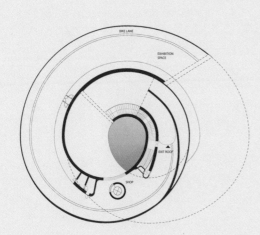

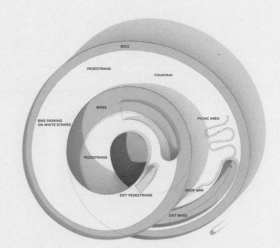

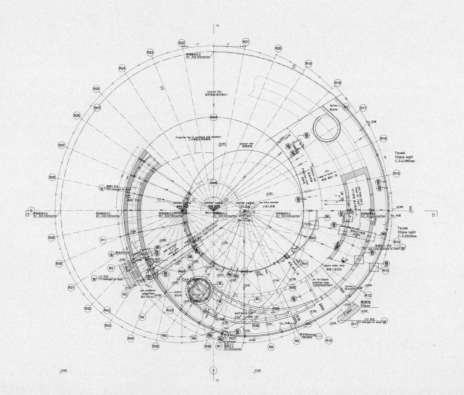

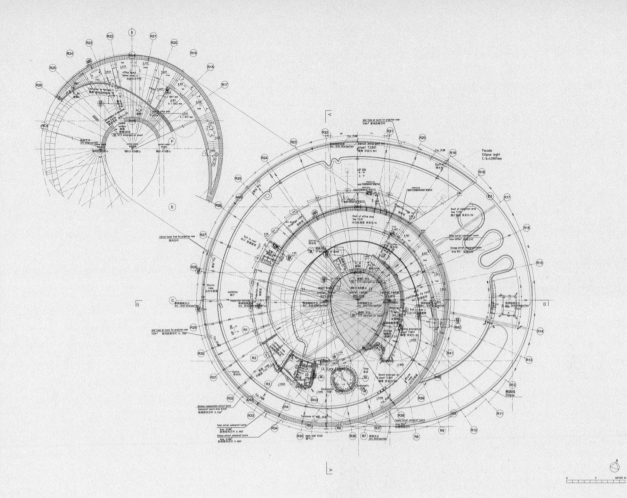

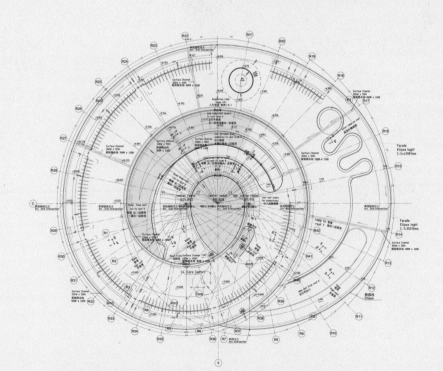

LUXEMBOURG PAVILION

Architects
Hermann & Valentiny

Theme
Small is Beautiful

Area
3,000 square meters

Location
Zone C, Expo Site

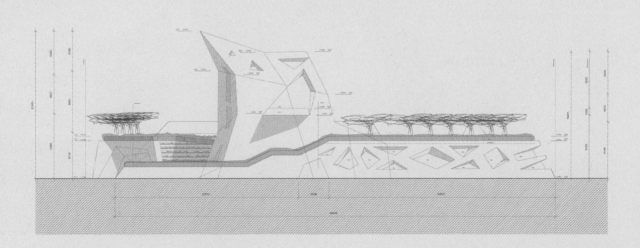

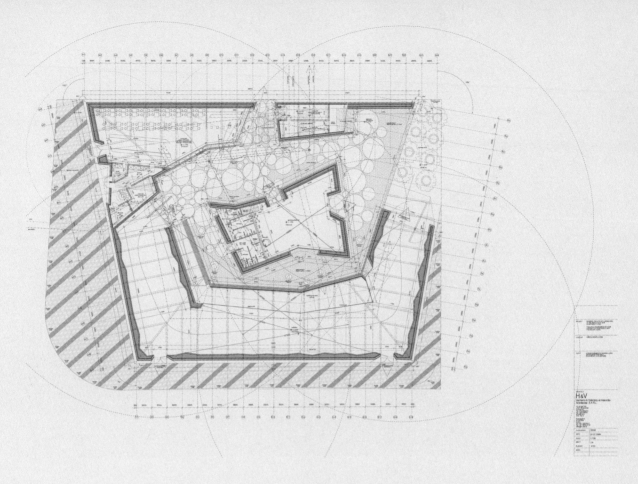

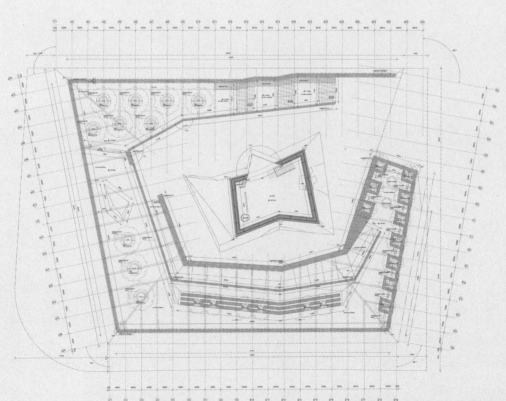

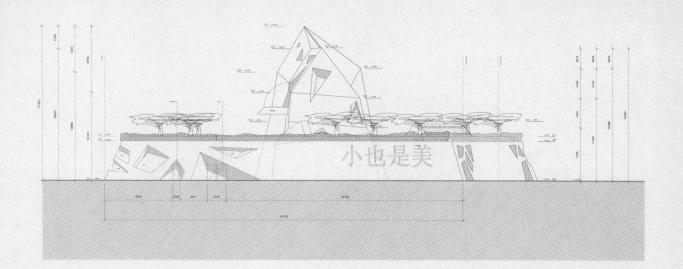

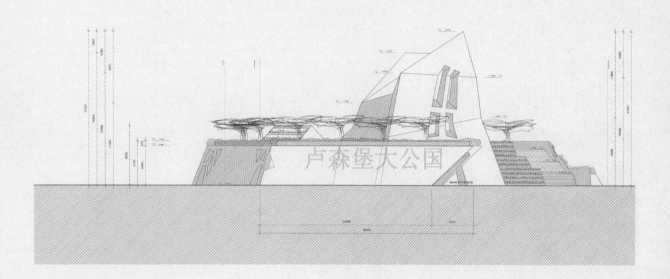

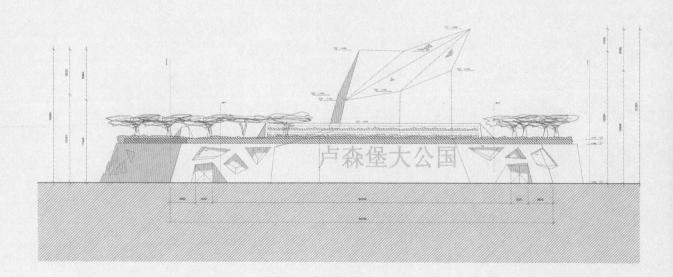

germany.

GERMAN PAVILION

Architects
Schmidhuber + Kaindl GmbH

Theme
Balancity

Area
6,000 square meters

Location
Zone C, Expo Site

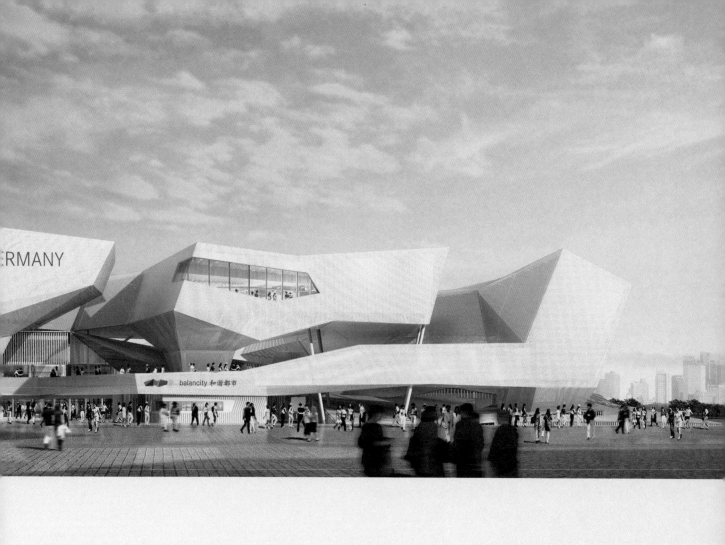

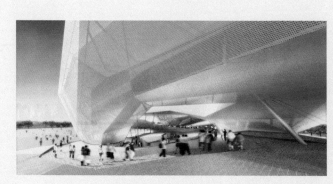

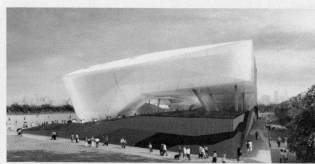

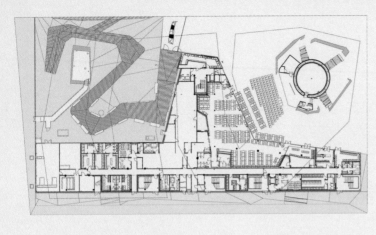

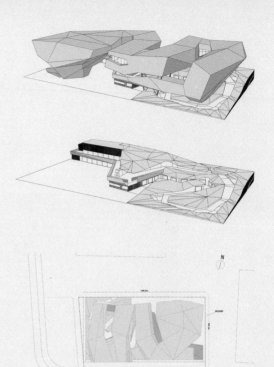

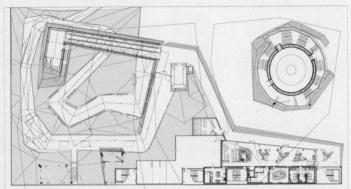

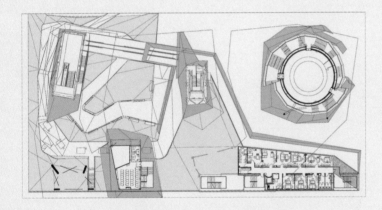

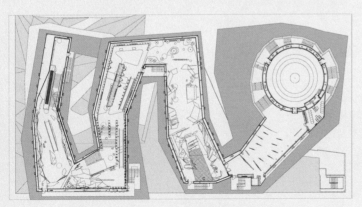

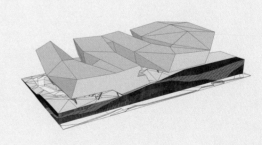

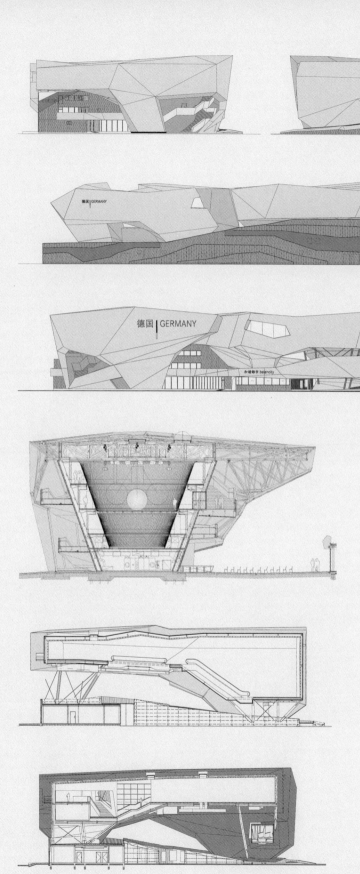

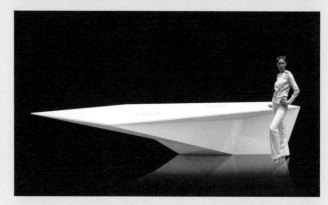

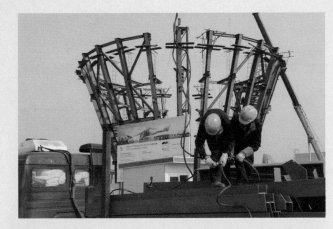

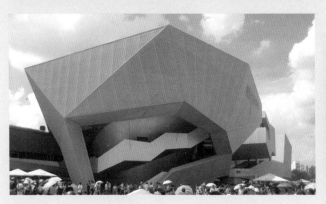

GERMAN – CHINESE HOUSE

Architects
Markus Heinsdorff

Theme
German-Chinese house

Area
350 square meters

Location
Zone C, Expo Site

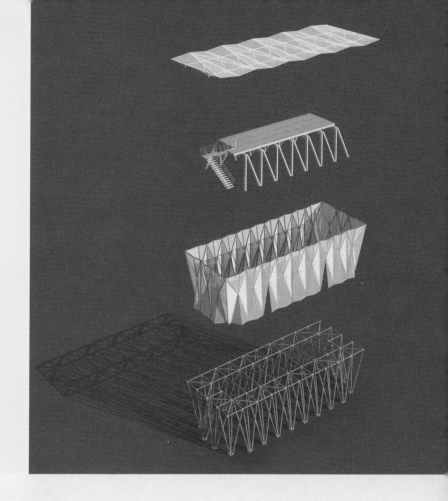

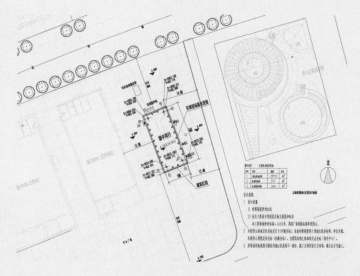

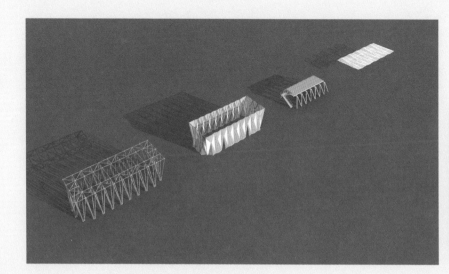

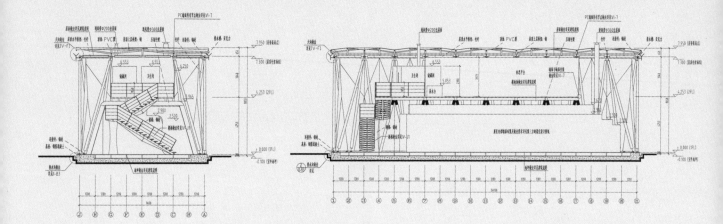

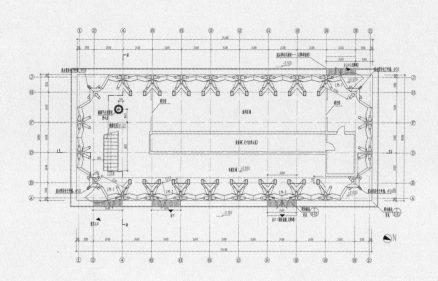

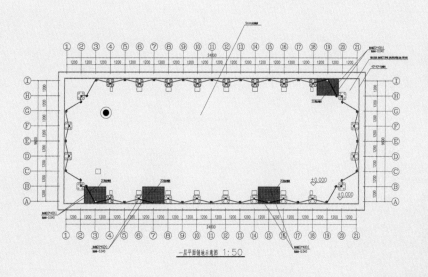

一层平面键地示意图 1:50

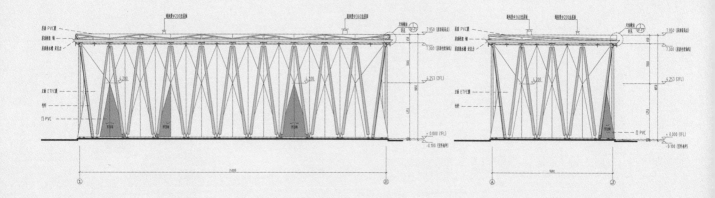

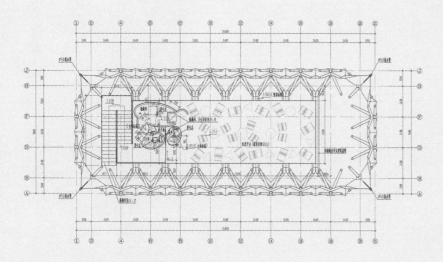

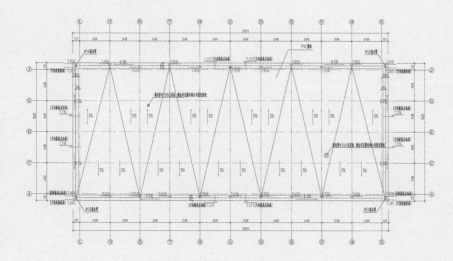

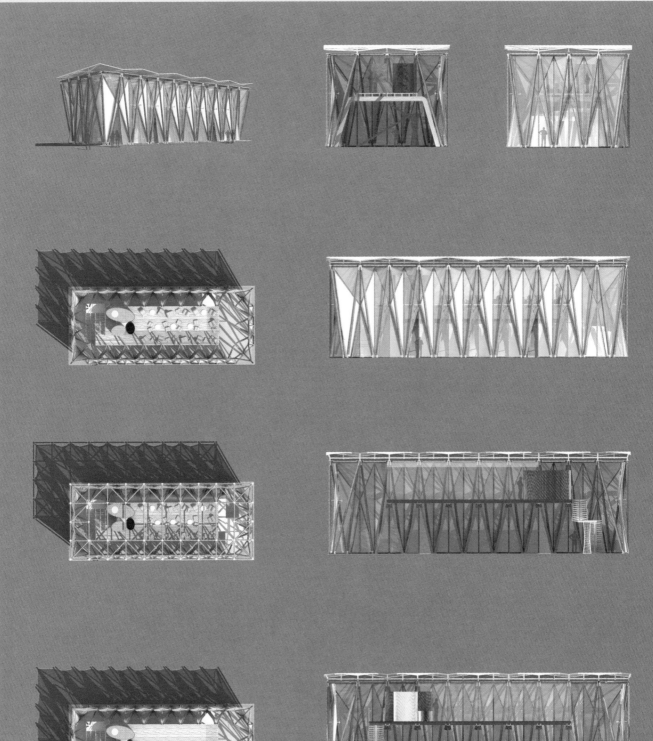

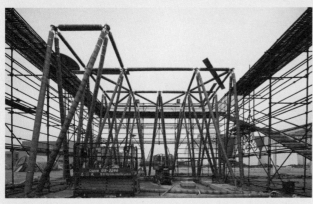

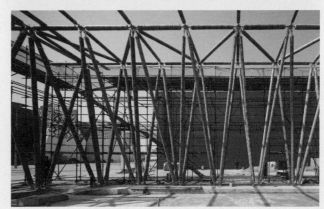

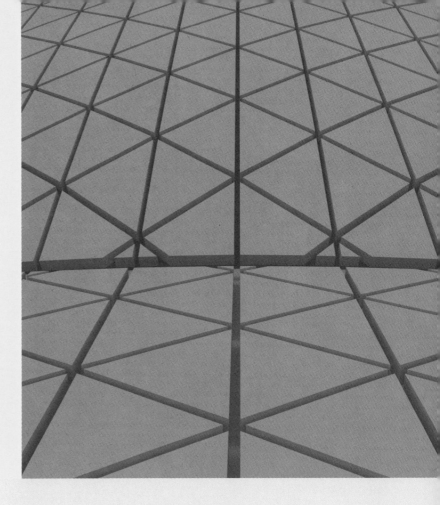

UNITED ARAB EMIRATES PAVILION

Architects
Foster + Partners

Theme
Power of Dreams

Area
6,000 square meters

Location
Zone A, Expo Site

uae.

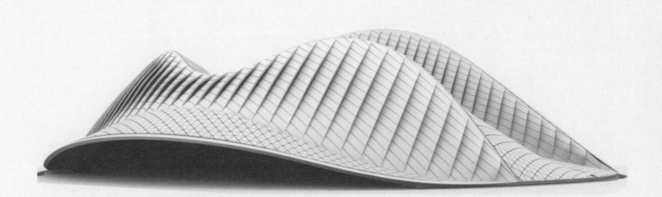

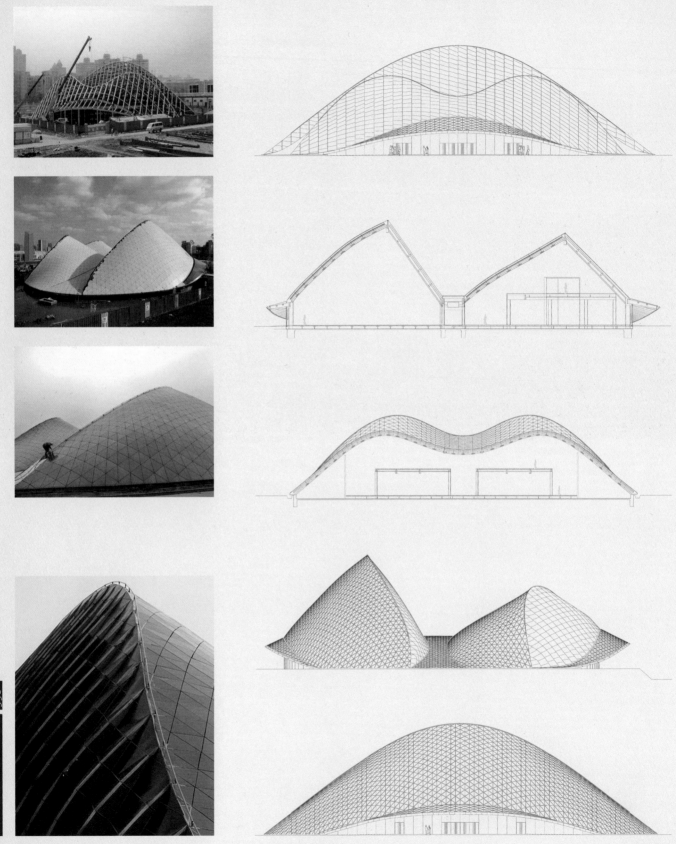

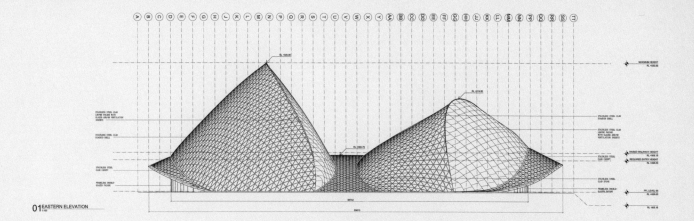

01 EASTERN ELEVATION

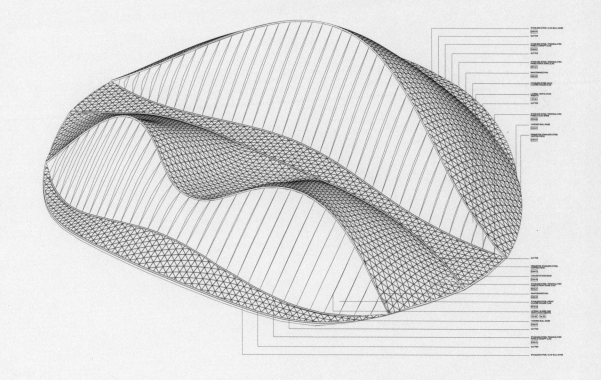

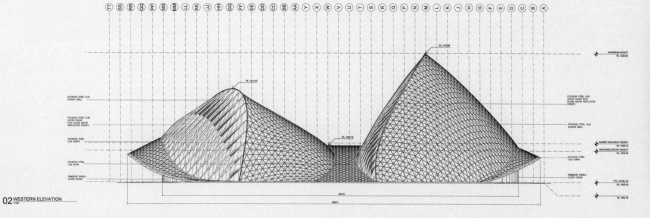

02 WESTERN ELEVATION

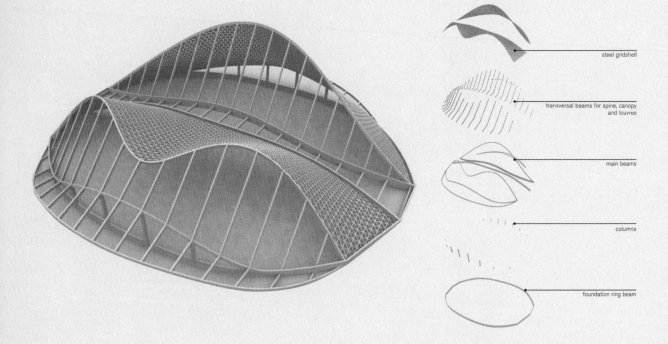

steel gridshell

transversal beams for spine, canopy
and louvres

main beams

columns

foundation ring beam

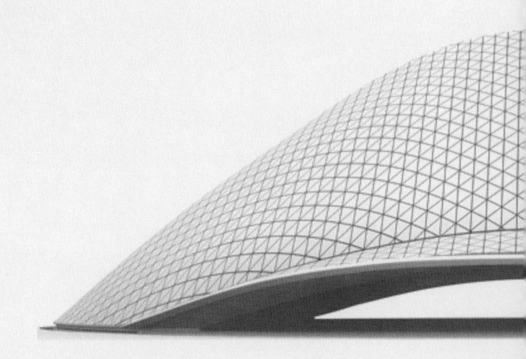

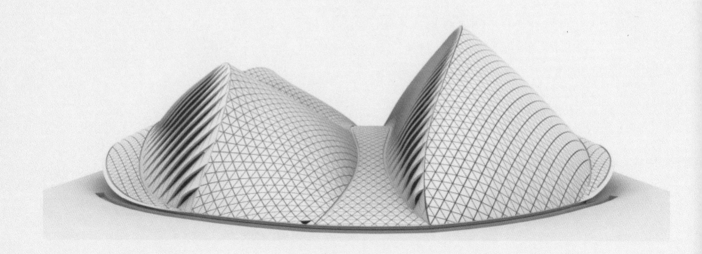

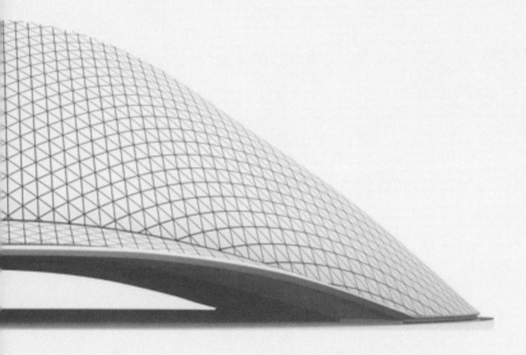

REPUBLIC OF KOREA PAVILION

Architects
Mass Studies

Theme
Friendly City, Colorful Life

Area
6,000 square meters

Location
Zone A, Expo Site

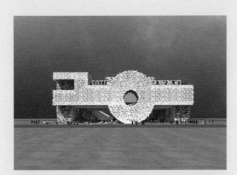

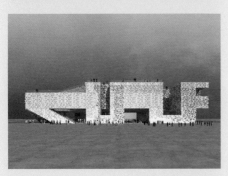

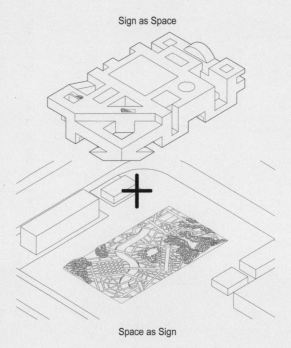

Sign as Space

Space as Sign

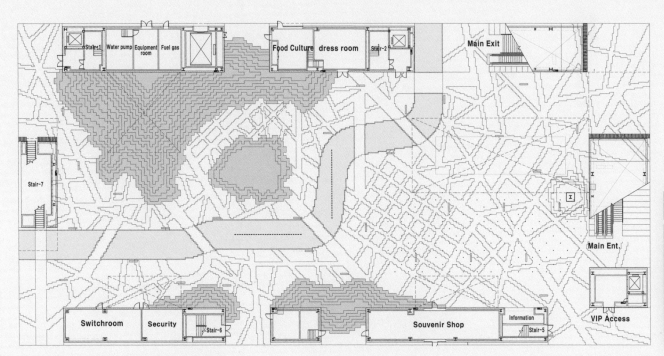

Korean City

Seoul in Shanghai

Space as Sign - 2D

Space as Sign - 3D

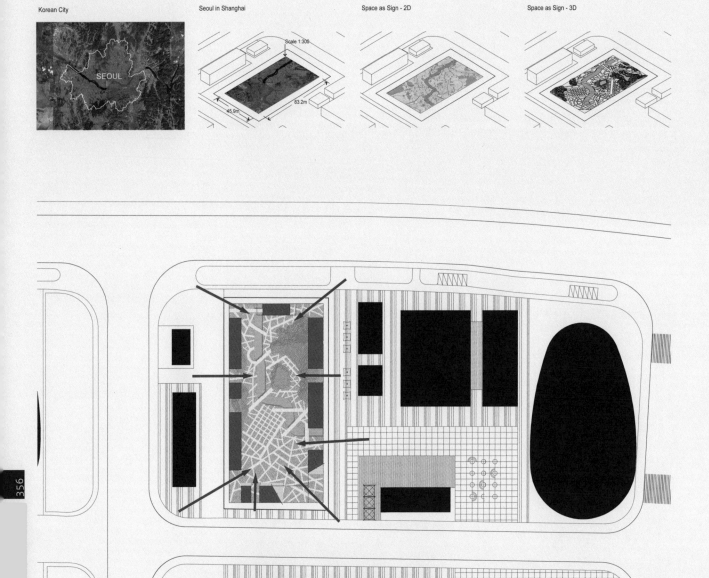

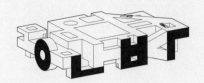
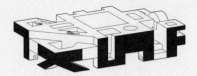
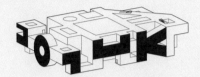
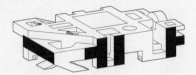
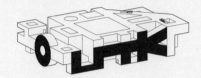

1. Program & Queue Line

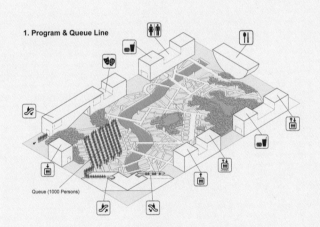

Queue (1000 Persons)

2. Interactive Media

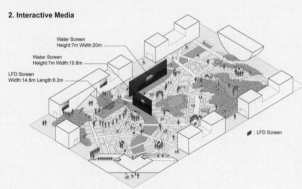

Water Screen
Height:7m Width:20m

Water Screen
Height:7m Width:10.8m

LFD Screen
Width:14.8m Length:6.3m

: LFD Screen

Leisure

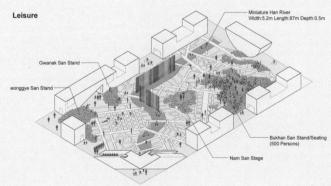

Miniature Han River
Width:5.2m Length:87m Depth:0.5m

Gwanak San Stand

eonggye San Stand

Bukhan San Stand/Seating
(500 Persons)

Nam San Stage

4. Event

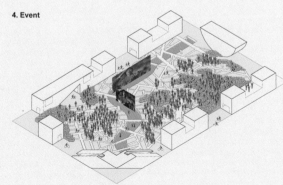

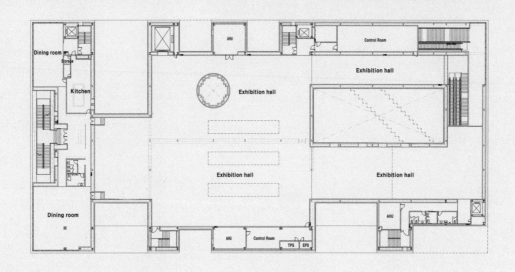

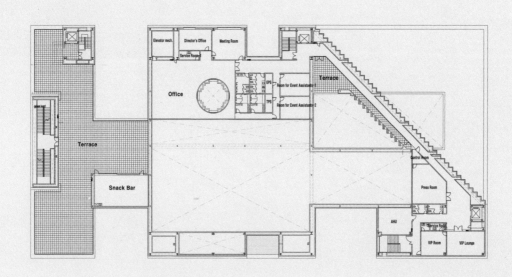

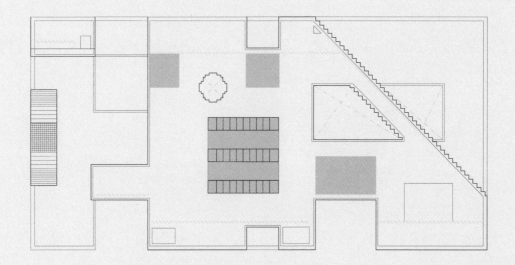

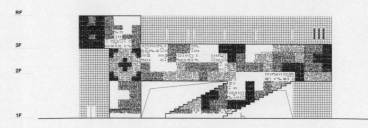

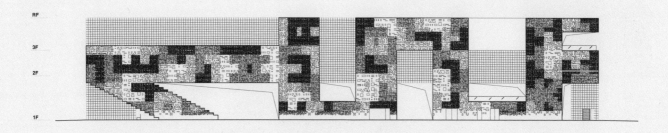

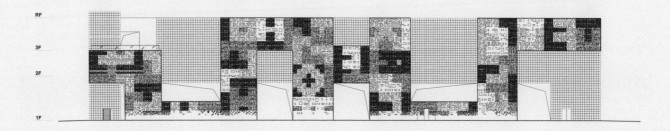

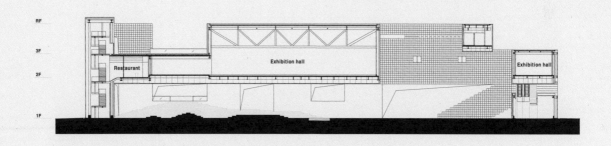

Restaurant

Exhibition hall

Exhibition hall

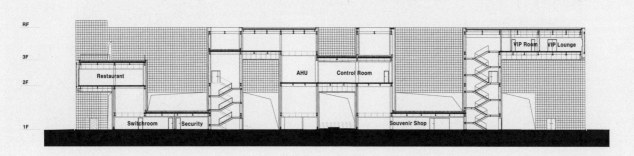

Restaurant

VIP Room | VIP Lounge

AHU | Control Room

Switchroom | Security

Souvenir Shop

0   5   10   15m

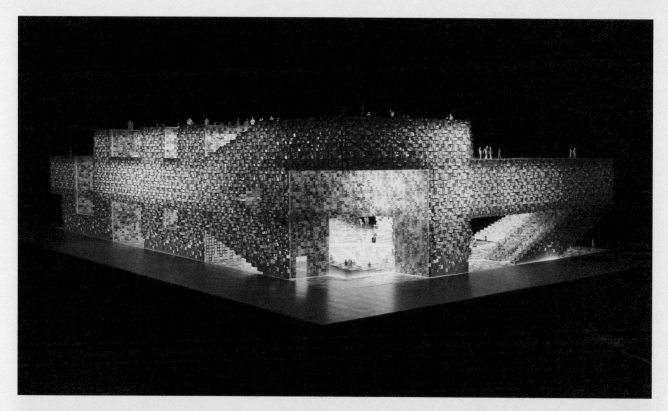

MAGIC CUBE -
SHANGHAI CORPORATE

Architects
Atelier Feichang Jianzhu

Theme
My City, Our Dreams

Area
4,949 square meters

Location
Zone D, Expo Site

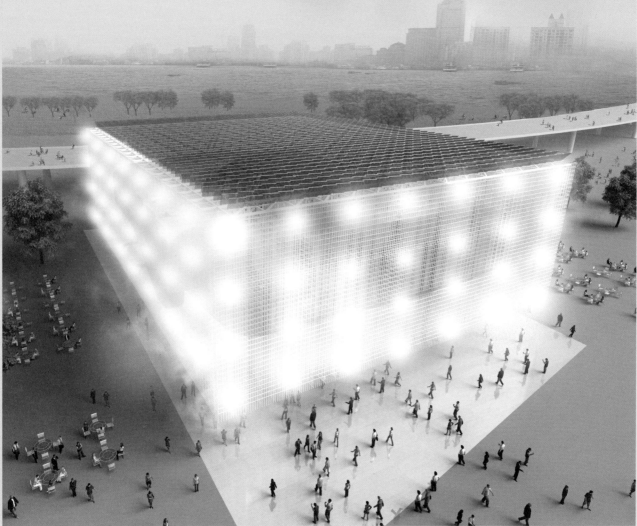

welcome to the SHANGHAI CORPORATE PAVILION
<<< ticketed guests
<< 企业联合馆
上海企业联合馆
《 企业联合馆》
企业联合馆》
general admission>>> VIP guests>>>

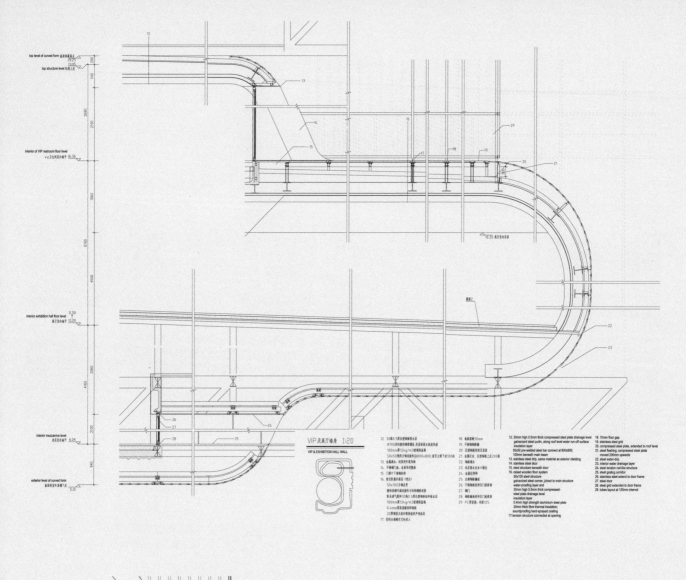

top level of curved form 顶点标高曲墙顶点 19.25
19.05
top structure level 结构之上 540
200

interior of VIP restroom floor level
vip3休闲室内立面 16.36

interior exhibition hall floor level
展厅室内地平 11.50
10.20

interior mazzanine level
夹层室内地平 6.04

exterior level of curved form
曲墙体墙下室内室墙下 27
5.10

2150
2990
1660
6160
4500
2380
4160
2100
940

12. 30和0.5厚压型钢板泄水层
φ100水沟铝钢管排管 其屋面沿水流度快道
50x50预焊主钢连接件800x800，双五上部下或100右
100mm 下或主梁
13. 金属底水、松皮材料系等外
14. 不锈钢滴水、在泵用列垂板
15. 门框下了穿钢板件
16. 朱空架基木屋架（竹片）
    50×100立钢板件
    楼拱角钢件与结连直部与钢钢钢钢水口
    防水基灶及度10和0.5厚压型钢板泄水层
    100mm 下或主梁上200隔热层
    0.4mm屏高强铝铝铝钢品
    2C罩硬灰无起经高硬度产由品层
17. 拉杆云起键经支处灯入

18. 南屋室内地坪10mm
19. 不锈钢网格
20. 不锈钢网水沟系竟
21. 全属泄水、在泵钢连上及200mm
22. 楼板泄水
23. 内层保温在层主门罐发
24. 金属层泄平
25. 在泵钢墙钢层
26. 钢结构层钢门铝上及其
27. 不锈钢格板被延度门框架
28. 铜棒板棒泄度
29. PC罩型板、间距125

VIP及展厅墙身 1:20
VIP & EXHIBITION HALL WALL

12. 30mm high 0.5mm thick compressed steel plate drainage level
    galvanized steel purlin, along roof level water run-off surface
    insulation layer
    50x50 pre-welded steel bar connect at 800x800;
    100mm beneath main beam
13. stainless steel drip, same material as exterior cladding
14. stainless steel drip
15. steel structure beneath door
16. raised wooden floor system
    50x100 steel structure
    galvanized steel corner, joined to main structure
    water-proofing layer and
    30mm high 0.5mm thick compressed
    steel plate drainage level
    insulation layer
    0.4mm high strength aluminium steel plate
    20mm thick fibre thermal insulation;
    soundproofing hard-sprayed coating
17. tension structure connected at opening

18. 10mm floor gap
19. stainless steel grid
20. compressed steel plate, extended to roof level
21. steel flashing, compressed steel plate
    moved 200mm upwards
22. steel water-drip
23. interior water drainage layer
24. steel tension net-like structure
25. steel grating corridor
26. steel grid extend to door frame
27. steel door
28. steel grid extended to door frame
29. tubes layout at 125mm interval

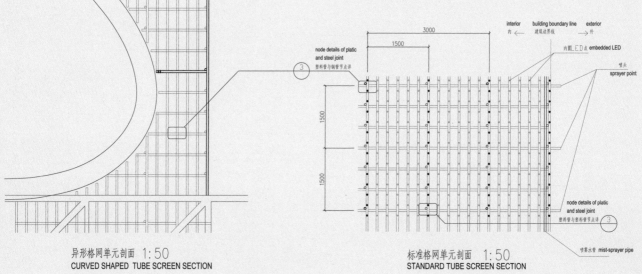

node details of platic
and steel joint
塑料管与铜管节点详 ③

异形格网单元剖面 1:50
CURVED SHAPED TUBE SCREEN SECTION

interior   building boundary line   exterior
内   建筑边界线   外

内面 LED点 embedded LED

喷头 sprayer point

node details of platic
and steel joint
塑料管与塑料管节点详 ③

喷雾水管 mist-sprayer pipe

3000
1500
1500
1500

标准格网单元剖面 1:50
STANDARD TUBE SCREEN SECTION

appendix.

credits.

370

expo axis pavilion

SBA GmbH is responsible for the overall planning design; expanded preliminary design of steel structure and membrane structure; conceptual design of interior and exterior landscape as well as the general guidance.

Invited Consulting of Membrane Structural Engineers: Knippers Helbig Advanced Engineering, Stuttgart/New York.

Invited Consulting of Ecological Techniques: Scholze Consulting GmbH, Leinfelden-Echterdingen.

Cooperate Partner: ECADI, Shanghai and SMEDI,Shanghai are responsible for engineering of architecture and structure, the development design of electromachine and construction drawing design.

Constructor: Shanghai World Expo Land Holding Co.,Ltd.

Credits of SBA GmbH: Li Hong, Bianca Nitsch, Cathrin Fischer, Reinhardt Braun, Zhang Lei, Qi Yijun.

chilean pavilion

Client: Government of the Republic Of Chile.

General Manager: Hernán Somerville S.

Architects: Sabbagh Arquitectos.
Juan Sabbagh P., Mariana Sabbagh P., Juan Pedro Sabbagh B. (Chief Architect), Felipe Sabbagh B.

Team: Marcelo Bastias V., Angeles Ferrada W.

Creative and Production: El Otro Lado.

Lighting: Diav.

Art Director: Rodrigo Bazaes. / Cristian Reyes.

Constructor: Shanghai Art Designing Corp.

spanish pavilion

Client: SEEI (State Society for International Exhibitions).

Principal in Charge: Benedetta Tagliabue.

PROJECT TEAM

Competition's Project Director: Mak oto Fukuda, Arch, Salvador Gilabert, Arch.

Project Director: Salvador Gilabert, Arch.

CONSTRUCTION

Project Director: Salvador Gilabert, Arch.

Project Director on Site: Igor Peraza, Arch.

Collaborators (Miralles Tagliabue EMBT): Makoto Fukuda, Guile Amadeu, Mattia Cappelletti, Vaiva Simoliunaite, Jack O'Kelly, Qiwei Hu, Gabriele Rotelli, Stefan Geenen, Paola Lodi, Cristina Salvi, Mireia Soriano, Travis McCarra, Lin Chia Ping, Lee Shun Chieh, Daniela Bortz, Barbara Asnaghi, Roberto Stefano Naboni, Carolina Carvalho, Maria Francesca Origa, Alessandra Deidda, Giuseppe Maria Fanara, Alice Puleo, Ailyn Alfaro, Jose Antonio Pavon, Armando Arteaga, Françoise Lempereur, Logan Yuen, Gordon Tannhauser, Xavier Ferrús, Fernanda Riotto Fernández, Paul Andrew Brogna, Ewa Pic, Christian Pàmies, Susana Osés, Verena Vogler, Clara Nubiola, Maria Loucaidou, Virginia Chiapas, Sara Cuccu, Jorge Andrés Cantor, Luis Alejandro Vivas, Giovanni Cetto, Simona Covello, Francesca Ciprini, Judith Plas, Gitte Kjaer, Natalia Leone, Michael Gonzales, Jan Kokol, Manuel Rearte, Kazuya Morita, Gian Mario Tonossi, Johane Ronsholt, Olivia Kostika, Cesar Trujillo, Carles Pastor, Marta Martinez, Noelia Pickard, Diego Parra, Ermanno Marota, Georgia Cetto, Guillermo Marcondes Zambrano, Guto Santos, Kirsti Øygarden, Luciana Cardoso, Marco Quagliantini, Michelangelo Pinto, Michele Buizza, Phuoc Tan Huynh.

Structural Engineers: Julio Martinez Calzón MC2 Structures Survey Engineering.

Mechanical Engineers: Tongji – The Architectural Design and Research Institute of Tongji University, PGI - Engineering.

Interior Designers: Miralles Tagliabue EMBT.

Landscape Architects: Miralles Tagliabue EMBT.

General Contractor: Inypsa.

french pavilion

Client: Cofres SAS.

Project Manager: Algoe.

Architect and Set-Designer: Jacques Ferrier.

Project Manager: Pauline Marchetti.

Project Leader: Olivier Cornefert.

Site Leader Architect: Aurélien Pasquier.

Set-Design Project Leader: Anna Sanna.

Models: Stéphane Levraud.

Team: Stéphane Bauche, Laurent Blondeau, François Louis, Chloé De Quillacq, Alexandra Union, Caroline Vagner.

Digital Images Manager: Corentin Lespagnol.

Landscape Architect: Agence TER: Michel Hoessler, Olivier Philippe, Henri Bava.

Team: Lauren Lynn, Flore Baudelot, Isabelle Costy, François Egreteau.

Consultant Engineer: C&E Ingénierie, Jean-Marc Weill.

Graphic Design: Olivier Andreotti, Anna Ferrier.

Lighting Engineer: Georges Sexton Associates.

Set-Design Consultant: Scénos-Associés, Christophe Giraud.

H.Q.E. Consultant: Tribu, Alain Bornarel.

Fluids Consultant: Barbanel Ingénierie.

Acoustician: Peutz.

Design Institute: Architectural Design & Research Institute of Tongji University.

Additional Photography: ©Jacques Ferrier architectures/photo Luc Boegly (pages 18, 75, 82, 83, 298, and 299).

uk pavilion

Main Client: Foreign & Commonwealth Office.

Lead Designer: Heatherwick Studio.

Team: Thomas Heatherwick, Katerina Dionysopoulou, Robert Wilson, Andrew Taylor Peter Ayres, Stuart Wood, Ingrid Hu, Jaroslav Hulin, Chiara Ferrari, Ramona Becker.

Project Manager / Principal Contractor: Mace Group.

Principal Sub-Contractor: Suzhong.

Structural Engineer: Adams Kara Taylor.

Environmental Engineer: Atelier Ten.

Fire & Risk engineering: Safe Consulting.

Executive Architect: Architectural Design & Research Institute of Tongji University.

Supporting Architects: RHWL.

Quantity Surveyor: Davis Langdon & Seah.

Walkway Exhibition Design: Troika.

Tbc: Mike Smith Studio.

Content Advisory Team: Mark Jones, John Sorrell, David Adjaye.

Content Advisor: Philip Dodd.

Content Coordinator: Adriana Paice.

FUNDING

Sponsors - Public Sector: Foreign & Commonwealth Office; UK Trade & Investment; British Council; Department for Communities and Local Government Department for Environment, Food and Rural Affairs Department for Business, Innovation and Skills; England's Regional Development Agencies; Department for Culture, Olympics, Media and Sport.

Sponsors – Private Sector: AstraZeneca; Barclays; BP; Diageo; GKN.t.

Construction Photography: ©Daniele Mattioli (pages 305, 306, and 307).

finland pavilion

Client: Finpro, Helsinki, Finland.

Building Management: Lemcon China.

Chief Architect: Teemu Kurkela.

Project Architect: Eero Kontuniemi.

Architects: Marko Pulli, Edit Bajsz, Johanna Raukko.

Interior Architects: Päivi Meuronen, Tero Hirvonen.

Scale Models: Klaus Stolt.

Architecture and Engineering: SCSAD, Shanghai.

FINNISH ENGINEERING CONSULTANTS

Structural Engineer: Aaro Kohonen Oy.

HVAC Engineer: Climaconsult Oy.

Electrical Engineer: Projectus Team Oy.

Acustical Engineer: Akukon.

Exhibition Design: Muotohiomo, Fantasiarakenne, Partanen & Lamusuo Partnership.

Artist: Aimo Katajamäki.

danish pavilion

Client: Ebst.

Collaborators: 2+1, Arup Agu, Arup Shanghai, Tongji Design Institute, Ai Wei Wei, Jeppe Hein, Martin De Thurah, Peter Funch.

Creative Director: Bjarke Ingels.

Partner-In-Charge: Finn Norkjaer.

Team: Tobias Hjortdahl, Jan Magasanik, Claus Tversted, Henrick Poulsen, Niels Lund Petersen, Kamil Szoltysek, Sonja , Reisinger, Anders Ulsted, Jan Borgstrom, Pauline Lavie, Teis Draiby, Daniel Sundlin, Line Gericke, Armen Menendian, Karsten Hammer Hansen, Martin W. Mortensen, Kenneth Sorensen, Jesper Larsen, Anders Tversted.

luxembourg pavilion

Client: Le Gouvernement du Grand-Duché de Luxembourg and GIE_Luxembourg@ ExpoShanghai2010 Groupement d'intérêt économique.

Project Leader: Dipl.-Des. Arch. GG Kirchner.

Partners in Shanghai: Architectural Design & Research Institute of Tongji University.

SFECO-China Shanghai (Group) Corporation for foreign economic & technological cooperation Engineering & Construction CO.

Planners

Hermann & Valentiny and Partners
Luxembourg – Wien
Hermann & Valentiny and Partners
Architectes s.à.r.l.

office@hvp.lu | www.hvp.lu

Colleagues

Dipl.-Ing. Torsten Altmeyer
Dipl.-Ing. Oliver Arenz
Dipl.-Ing. Arch. Daniela Flor
Dipl.-Ing. Henning Kiefer
Dipl.-Des. Arch. GG. Kirchner
Richard Krecké
Marie-France Matz
Paul Majerus
Architekt D.E Olivier Vigneron
Dipl.-Ing. Arch. Wolfgang Weil.

Renderings: Oliver Arenz, HVP.

Plans: HVP.

german pavilion

Overall Responsibility: German Federal Ministry of Economics and Technology.

Organisation and Operation: Koelnmesse International GmbH.

Design, Planning and Realisation: Consortium German Pavilion Shanghai GbR.

Exhibition: Milla und Partner GmbH, Stuttgart.

Execution: Nüssli (Deutschland) GmbH, Roth.

Chief Architect: Lennart Wiechell.

Executive Director Consortium German Pavilion: Siegfried Kaindl.

Project Direction: Bernd Herrndorf.

Project Management Membrane: Florian Özdikmen.

Team: Julia Voormann, Tina Mühlbusch, Jan Domin, Udo Ribbe, Gerd Hermes, Stephanie Kobler, Maria Ostermayer, Christine Clöß.

Visualization: Benjamin Pächthold, Alexander Breier.

german-chinese house

Architectural Design: Chefarchitect Markus Heinsdorff, Munich Germany.

Cooperation with:

MUDI Architects Shanghai, China; planning execution together with Tongji University Shanghai, China, office for Architecture and Statics.

Tong Lingfeng, Architect Shanghai; assistant architectural Design.

Prof. Dr. -Ing. Mike Sieder VariCon, Technical University Munich, Germany, Chair of Timber Structures and Building Construction; Structural Design.

Prof. Dr. -Ing. Harald Garrecht, University of Technology Darmstadt, Germany, Institute of Solid and Construction and Prof. J. Schneider Materials in Civil Engineering; Connections.

Tebodin Consultants & Engineer, Shanghai, China, Construction Management.

Schlaich, Bergermann & Partner Stuttgart, Germany, Consulting Statics.

Oriental Expo Shanghai, China; implementation together with Oldenburg Shanghai; carpenters Workshop, Covertex, Shanghai; Membrane Structure.

City Interactive Game: Technical University Aachen, Germany.

Construction Photography: Kingkay, Architectural Photographer (pages 344, 345, 346, and 347).

uae pavilion

Client: National Media Council.

Structural Engineers:
Halvorson and Partners.

M&E: PHA.

Lighting: Claude Engle.

Local Architect: ECADI.

south korea pavilion

Client: Korea Trade-Investment Promotion Agency.

Architects: Mass Studies.

Minsuk Cho, Kisu Park, Joungwon Lee, Taehoon Hwang, Hyunseok Jung, Joonhee Lee, Hyunjung Kim, Bumhyun Chun, Jisoo Kim, Moonhee Han, Sungpil Won, Kyungmin Kwon, Dongwon Yoon, Betty Bora Kim, Kyehnyong Kwak, Jungwook Lee, Doohyun An.

Construction Drawings: NIKKO.

Structural Engineer: SD: Ove Arup & Partners / CD: NIKKO.

MEP Engineer: NIKKO.

Façades Consultant: Axis Facades.

Finishing Materials: Composite Aluminum Panels, EPDM Blocks.

Interior (Exhibition): Cheil Worldwide.

Multimedia: SigongTech.

shanghai corporate pavilion

Client: Shanghai Guosheng Group Co., Ltd.

Principal Architect: Yung Ho Chang.

Project Architect: Zang Feng.

Interior Architects: Liu Lubin, James Shen.

Project Team: Wong Siuming, Wang Kuan,Qiu Yukui, Liang Xiaoning, Wang Lin, Wu Xia, Zhang Minghui, Wu Jie,Chen Guannan,Tang Hung Fai.

Consultants: Center for Engineering Design and Research under the Headquarters of General Equipment.

Structure Material: Steel.

Executive Producer: Derong Shi, PhD.

Curator: Mary Gu.

Technical Director: Zhou Fengguang (Center for Engineering Design and Research under the Headquarters of General Equipment).

Exhibition Design: ESI Design (USA).

Director: Don Mischer (USA).

Executive Producer: David Goldberg (USA).

Lighting Design: Full Flood inc. (USA).

Media Design: Spinifex Group (AUS).

Rodolphe El-Khoury

Rodolphe el-Khoury is Canada Research Chair in Architecture and Urban Design at the University of Toronto and partner in the design firm Khoury Levit Fong. He is the author of numerous critically acclaimed books in architectural history and theory and a regular contributor to professional and academic journals. His books include; *Monolithic Architecture, Architecture: in Fashion, Shaping the City; Studies in History, Theory and Urban Design*, and *See Through Ledoux, Architecture, Theatre, and the Pursuit of Transparency*. He has received several awards and international recognition for his design work at Office dA, ReK Productions and currently at KLF. el-Khoury is particularly interested in architectural applications for advanced information technology aimed at enhanced responsiveness and sustainability in the built environment.

Andy Payne

Andrew Payne is a Senior Lecturer at the Daniels Faculty of Architecture, Landscape, and Design at the University of Toronto, where he also teaches in the Literary Studies Program. His articles on architecture, art, and contemporary culture have appeared in publications like the *Harvard Design Magazine*, *Praxis*, *Public*, and *Parachute*. He is is also the author of numerous monograph and catalogue essays on various contemporary artists and architects. He is currently working on two book manuscripts. The first, *Thales or Some Other: The Intellectual and Cultural Legacies of Construction*, examines the significance of a single term, construction, in the modernization of the intellectual and cultural disciplines. He is also co-authoring a second book manuscript with Rodolphe el-Khoury, *Distributions of the Sensible: Architecture, The Reorganization of Sense Experience*, and *the Meaning of Modernity*. The book examines the successive recalibrations of the relationship between sense experience and cognition in architectural theory and practice from the seventeenth century to the present.

Nic Lehoux

Nic is a Canadian architectural photographer who constantly works with progressive architects who are pushing the boundaries in design of the built environment.
Nic is regularly commissioned around the world to document significant buildings with his unique eye, lighting and sense of composition. His images are regularly published in the international architectural press.
Concurrently to his professional work, Nic has made several visits to West Africa to document the People and Architecture of the Sahel. He is also working on several books of personal work, generally concerned with theca transitional evolution of the built environment and the people within it. One of these projects is titled 'Detritus: Explorations in a Marginal Environment.' It documents the modern vestiges of abandoned industry, cities and buildings in North America and Europe. This 10 year long project showcases the impact and legacy of an industrial revolution which is in transition into the 21st century.
Amongst others, Nic's work is influenced very strongly by the concept of the 'decisive moment', popularized by Henri-Cartier-Bresson, but adapted to the rigors of architectural photography. His images therefore serve as a reflection on the interaction of people within the built environment.

Oscar Riera Ojeda

Oscar Riera Ojeda is an editor and designer based in Philadelphia, Singapore, and Buenos Aires. Born in 1966, in Argentina, he moved to the United States in 1990.
Since then he has published over one hundred books, assembling a remarkable body of work notable for its thoroughness of content, timeless character, and sophisticated and innovative craftsmanship.
Oscar Riera Ojeda's books have been published by many prestigious publishing houses across the world, including ORO editions, Birkhäuser, Byggförlaget, The Monacelli Press, Gustavo Gili, Thames & Hudson, Rizzoli, Whitney Library of Design, and Taschen.
Oscar Riera Ojeda is also the creator of numerous architectural book series, including Ten Houses, Contemporary World Architects, The New American House and The New American Apartment, Architecture in Detail, and Single Building.
His work has received many international awards, in-depth reviews, and citations.
He is a regular contributor and consultant for several publications in the field.
At the current time he is devoting most of his time to his own imprint called Oscar Riera Ojeda Publishers.

First published in the United Kingdom in 2010 by
Thames & Hudson Ltd, 181A High Holborn,
London WC1V 7QX

Copyright © 2010 by Oscar Riera Ojeda Publishers

Concept and Compilation by Oscar Riera Ojeda.
Creative Direction by Leo Malinow.
Graphic Design by Alejandra Román.
Copy Editing by Kit Maude.

www.oscarrieraojeda.com
info@oscarrieraojeda.com

British Library Cataloguing-in-Publication Data
A catalogue record for this book is available from the British Library

ISBN: 978-0-500-34269-5

Printed and bound in China

To find out about all our publications, please visit **www.thamesandhudson.com.**
There you can subscribe to our e-newsletter, browse or download our current catalogue, and buy any titles that are in print.